Adobe Premiere Elements 2025

Handbook for Beginners

A Comprehensive Step-By-Step Guide to Master Professional Video Creation and Editing

Rhett Lysander

TABLE OF CONTENTS

TABLE OF CONTENTS

CHAPTER 1
INTRODUCTION TO ADOBE PREMIERE ELEMENTS

What is Adobe Premiere Elements?

For those who aren't quite ready to take their video editing skills to the next level, Adobe Premiere Elements is an intuitive and easy-to-use program. It's a streamlined version of Adobe Premiere Pro that still has all the features experienced editors need, but is easier to use for beginners. The UI is designed to be user-friendly, providing choices for users of all skill levels to easily navigate the editing process. You can choose between Quick, Guided, and advanced editing modes in Premiere Elements. If you need to quickly rearrange clips, create transitions, or make a movie, the Quick mode is where it's at. If you're just starting, the Guided mode is a lifesaver. It walks you through common editing tasks like clip trimming, transitioning, and title creation. Those who wish to fine-tune their edits to a higher degree have additional options in the Advanced mode.

Among Premiere Elements' notable features is its automatic editing tools, such as Auto Creations, which can take your photographs and clips and turn them into shareable videos. Smart Trim simplifies and speeds up the editing process by automatically analyzing your film and selecting the best moments based on quality, faces, and activity. You can also use the software's motion tracking feature to overlay moving text or images on top of a video. A variety of transitions and effects, like slow-motion, animated overlays, and chroma key (green screen), are available in Premiere Elements to improve your projects. You can also use the integrated audio tools to add music, voiceovers, and sound effects, and to tweak the volume and EQ. Premiere Elements' Organizer feature makes it easy to arrange and locate video files, which is useful for applications beyond just editing. The program also facilitates sharing by providing choices to export films in device-specific formats or to post them straight to sites like Vimeo and YouTube. In general, Adobe Premiere Elements is designed to make video editing fun and easy by providing just the correct amount of power and simplicity so that anybody can generate films that appear professional.

New Features in the 2025 Edition

An easy-to-use video editing tool, Adobe Premiere Elements 2025 streamlines the process of making professional-quality films. Several improvements and new features are included in the 2025 version.

They include:

- **Dynamic Title Creation**: With the new and enhanced text styling tools, users can now create dynamic titles that are visually appealing and easy to edit in terms of alignment, color, and size. This will greatly improve video presentations.

- **Enhanced Color Correction Tools**: With the new white balance tool and color correction curves, users can fine-tune colors to ensure their film has consistent and realistic hues. This is part of the enhanced color correction tools.

- **Creative Color Grading with LUTs**: Premiere Elements 2025 now has support for Lookup Tables (LUTs), which allow for the creative use of color grading presets. This allows users to quickly change the style and mood of films.
- **Simplified Timeline Navigation**: Video and audio tracks are now grouped on the timeline, making navigating much easier. To avoid inadvertent modifications, you can lock specific tracks and use the new Quick Tools menu to access often-used editing tools.
- **Access to Free Adobe Stock Title Templates**: Users have access to free Adobe Stock title templates that come in a range of styles to fit different video themes. These templates can be used to enhance production.
- **Apple M3 Chip Support**: The program is designed to work quicker on Mac computers that are compatible with Apple's M3 processor.
- **Web and Mobile Companion Apps (Beta)**: Premiere Elements 2025 brings companion apps for online and mobile platforms. These apps let users add moving overlays, modify backgrounds, and adjust light and color using sliders. They make editing on the move much easier.

By simplifying the process of video editing and providing creative freedom, these capabilities make Adobe Premiere Elements 2025 a flexible tool for users of all skill levels.

System Requirements and Installation

For Adobe Premiere Elements 2025 to run at its best, your computer has to have these specs:

Windows

- **Processor:** Intel 6th Generation or newer, or AMD equivalent with SSE4.2 support.
- **Operating System:** Microsoft Windows 10 (version 22H2) or Windows 11 (version 23H2); 64-bit versions only.
- **Memory:** 8 GB of RAM.
- **Storage:** 10 GB of available hard-disk space for installation; additional space required for downloading online content and for temporary files during installation and usage.
- **Display Resolution:** 1440 x 900 resolution (at 100% scale factor).
- **Graphics:** 4 GB of GPU VRAM.
- **Additional Requirements:** An Internet connection is required for product activation and download of online content.

macOS

- **Processor:** Intel 6th Generation or newer; Apple silicon M1 or newer.
- **Operating System:** macOS 13, macOS 14 (14.4 or later).

- **Memory:** 8 GB of RAM.
- **Storage:** 15 GB of available hard-disk space for installation; additional space required for downloading online content and for temporary files during installation and usage.
- **Display Resolution:** 1440 x 900 resolution (at 100% scale factor).
- **Graphics:** 4 GB of GPU VRAM.
- **Additional Requirements:** An Internet connection is required for product activation and download of online content.

Installation Steps

1. **Download the Installer:**
   - Visit the Adobe Premiere Elements download page.
   - Sign in with your Adobe ID.
   - Select the appropriate version for your operating system and click "Download."
2. **Run the Installer:**
   - **Windows:**
     - Navigate to your downloads folder.
     - Double-click the downloaded .exe file.
   - **macOS:**
     - Navigate to your downloads folder.
     - Double-click the downloaded .dmg file.
     - In the window that opens, double-click the "Install" icon.
3. **Follow On-Screen Instructions:**
   - Sign in with your Adobe ID when prompted.
   - Choose the installation location and language preferences.
   - Click "**Install**" to begin the process.
4. **Complete Installation:**
   - Allow the installation to finish.
   - Once completed, launch Adobe Premiere Elements 2025.
   - If you have a redemption code, enter it when prompted to activate the software.

Understanding the User Interface

Those who enjoy working with video will find the Adobe Premiere Elements workspace to be user-friendly. It categorizes features according to their level of complexity, offering Quick, Guided, and Advanced views.

Home screen

The Home screen is the initial screen that appears when you start Adobe Premiere Elements. Launch the app of your choice, peruse a variety of feature tutorials, find resources for the most recent features, peruse Auto Creations, and much more from this screen.

Views

There are three distinct perspectives in Adobe Premiere Elements' workspace, each with its own set of editing tools. Start with **Quick** and **Guided**. After you've gotten the hang of things, go over the **Advanced** view's potent tools.

Quick View

Streamline your video editing and sharing with **Quick View**, which compiles the essential tools that enthusiasts rely on. It streamlines typical clip operations like editing and sharing videos. Titles, effects, transitions, and background music can be added to your video using the **Quick View** options. If you need a cleaner video, you can utilize Smart Trim, pan the camera, or zoom in.

Quick view sceneline

Premiere Elements 2025's Quick View sceneline features a "V1" track and an audio-video track, much like any other real sceneline. You can only use the V2 track for video files, and the A1 track for audio files. The mouse menu also allows you to add or remove songs. To access the smart trim workspace, simply click the **Edit video clip** button on any video. From there, you can remove any unneeded bits from individual clips. One way to create a logical movie sequence is to move video clips around. At the beginning or finish of your media, or between two media, you can also apply transition effects. The Audio tracks also allow you to record narration or music to add to your film.

Guided Edit View

You can learn to edit videos progressively through several stages in the Guided view. Improve your video clips with the aid of guided edits, which allow you to do things like remove unnecessary material and add animations to your graphics.

Advanced View

For complex video editing jobs, pros employ the additional features and tools included in the Advanced view, such as Audio Mixer. The Advanced view includes the Project Assets panel in addition to the Quick view's panels. The media files that you bring into your Premiere Elements project are housed in this panel. Choose between a list and a grid view for the files using the panel's choices. With the grid view, you can get a little preview of every file. Below the thumbnail of each media item, you'll see a blue indicator that indicates its addition to the timeline.

Advanced View timeline

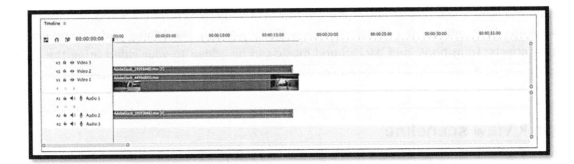

Use the Advanced View timeline for more complex editing. The timeline in the advanced view shows your film project visually as a series of vertically stacked tracks containing video and audio snippets. The video segments play again in the order they happened when recorded with a digital video recorder. You can see how your movie's elements interact with one another over time in the Advanced View timeline, which makes use of a time ruler. Scenes can be added or removed, markers can be used to highlight key frames, transitions can be added, and the blending or superimposition of clips can be controlled. The timeline's right-click options are neatly categorized for easy access. The Advanced view timeline has more tracks than the Quick view.

Quick Tools panel in advanced view

Inside the **Advanced view Timeline** panel, you'll find several shortcut keys and buttons that you can use to quickly access various tools. You can see the name and shortcut for a tool when you hover over it.

Selection Tool

Clips, menu items, and other UI components are often selected with the **Selection Tool**. After you've done using a more specialized tool, it's usually a good idea to go to the **Selection Tool**.

Track Selection Forward Tool

Pick a clip and all clips to the right in their track. With a **Shift-click**, you can choose not just the clip but also all clips on the right side of the track. The Track Selection Tool becomes the Multi-track Selection Tool when you press **Shift**.

Track Selection Backward Tool

Choose a clip; the ones on the left are already in their respective tracks. With a **Shift-click**, you can choose not just the clip but also any clips to its left in all tracks. The Track Selection Tool becomes the Multi-track Selection Tool when you press **Shift**.

Ripple Edit Tool

Within a timeline, you can use this tool to change the in/out point of a clip. After you trim a clip, the **Ripple Edit Tool** will fill in any gaps it leaves behind while preserving any previous adjustments that were made before or after it.

Rate Stretch Tool

You can change the playback speed of a clip in Premiere Elements using the **Rate Stretch Tool**. You can speed it up to make it shorter or slow it down to make it longer. This tool is great since it keeps the original **in** and **out** points of the clip.

Scissor

Cut off specific segments of video from a **timeline** with this handy tool. To split a clip at a given moment, you must first choose that point. While holding down Shift, you can split clips in all tracks at that place by simply selecting the area in any of the clips.

Text Tool

In the **Program** window, use this tool to insert horizontal text into the clip.

Remix Tool

When you use this feature in Premiere Elements, you won't have to spend as much time trimming, tweaking, applying fades, and screening your work in an attempt to get the music to match the scene length.

Rectangle Tool

In the **Program** window, you can use this tool to draw a rectangle within the clip. I would like to suggest the Polygon and Ellipsis tools as well.

Add

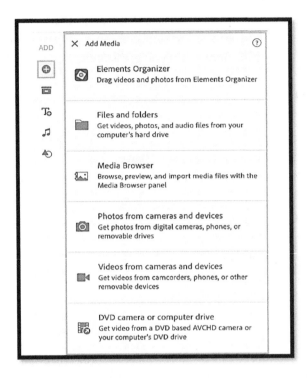

Add Media

You can add media files using the Add Media panel. Elements Organizer, Files and folders, Media Browser, and media captured by cameras and other devices are all viable options for adding media files.

Project Assets

You can preview project assets in the **Project Assets** panel, which is accessible in both the **Guided** and **Advanced** views. Project Assets will be accessible when you choose either the **Guided** or **Advanced** view.

Titles

You can find title templates that are already prepared and ready to use in your movie by clicking the **title** button.

Music

Allows you to add theme music to your movie

Graphics

You can add visual elements, such as clip art, to your movies to make them more appealing. This feature is available in both the Guided and Advanced views.

Graphics panel for Premiere Elements 2025

Export & Share

You can find all the tools you need to export and share your completed project in the **Export & Share** panel. You have the option to save your project for viewing on many platforms, including the web, mobile phones, computers, DVDs (for versions 2022 and previous), and Blu-ray discs. A consolidated panel displaying all export formats is provided by the **Export & Share** option. The many media possibilities are represented by individual tabs on the **Export & Share panel**. The **Export & Share** panel is where you can go to export your finished creation for sharing.

Toolbar

Premiere Elements organizes all of its editing controls and tools into three groups on the right panel, according to the functions they perform:

Fix

Adjust

You can change the clip's basic characteristics, such as its color and lighting, via the Adjust section. You can use the Adjust panel to change the attributes of your clip's title if you need to.

Tools

Offers options that let you add cool effects to your video. Time remapping is one tool you can utilize to provide your videos with professional-level motion effects. Select Smart Trim to have Premiere Elements do the automatic trimming for you, resulting in a cleaner final product.

Edit

Effect Controls

Provides access to the details of effects that have been applied to your video. The panel offers a range of choices that let you adjust the effects that have been applied.

Effects

Displays the available presets and special effects for use with your movie clips. After applying a special effect, you can alter its properties in the Effect Controls panel by clicking Effect Controls. The Advanced View offers a more comprehensive set of effects that are arranged into several categories than the Quick view.

Transitions

Offers transitions that can be utilized to link your video clips together. When you initially apply a transition, the Transition contextual control will show automatically. Make use of it to alter the transition characteristics. After you double-click the transition, the contextual control will open. There are more transition effects available in the Advanced View than in the Quick view.

Action bar

You can access these settings from the Action bar:

Undo

Undoes the previous action.

Redo

Repeats the action performed.

Organizer

Opens Elements Organizer to let you organize and manage your media files.

Home Screen

Launches the home screen of Premiere Elements

Events panel

You can find and fix issues, especially those related to third-party components and plug-ins, by perusing the warnings and error messages shown in the Events panel. If there is an issue, you will see an alert icon △, ⊗, ⍓ on the status bar. The Events panel can be accessed by double-clicking the icon, and the status bar icon can be removed from the panel by removing the related item.

1. **Do either of the following:**
    - o Double-click the **Alert** icon in the status bar.
    - o Select **Window** > **Events**.
2. **Do any of the following:**
    - o To learn more about an item in the list, select **Details**.
    - o To clear the events list, select **Clear All**.

Event notification

Notification windows spring up in the bottom right corner of the user interface and the Events panel both display alert icons. For a brief moment, a notice will show up; the color of the notification's background denotes the kind of occurrence. A red background indicates an error, a yellow background indicates a caution and a blue background indicates information. As a default, the notification pop-up window will display. To disable it, go to the Preferences menu and find the General category. Deselect **Show Event Indicator.**

Info panel

Details about the selected clip's file are displayed in the **Info panel**. Pick a timeline clip or project object to open it, after going to **Window > Info.** Under the timeline's current-time indicator, the Info panel shows details about the item you've chosen as well as the timecode information for the clips. The panel's top section displays information relevant to the current selection. The sort of media it is, the active panel, and other factors determine how this data is presented.

- **Video:** Indicates frame rate, frame size, and pixel aspect ratio in that order.
- **Audio:** Indicates sample rate, bit depth, and channels in that order.
- **Tape:** Indicates the name of the tape.
- **In:** Indicates the Inpoint timecode of the selected clip.
- **Out:** Indicates the Outpoint timecode of the selected clip.
- **Duration:** Indicates the duration of the selected clip.

Using the new features

Titles with text controls

Create dynamic titles with text styling controls

Motion Graphics templates (MOGRTs) give Premiere Elements editors the power of After Effects motion graphics, packaged up as templates with easy-to-use controls designed to be customized in Premiere Elements. The Type and Shape tools in Premiere Elements allow users to easily design new titles and graphics. These can then be exported as Motion Graphics templates, making them easy to reuse or share. There are pre-made Motion Graphics templates in Premiere Elements that were made in After Effects and Premiere Pro. **Additional sources for importing Motion Graphics templates into Premiere Elements are:**

- Adobe Stock
- Your local folders

Install Motion Graphics templates

You can install a Motion Graphics template from your computer and put it into the folder in the Titles and Shapes panel. You won't find Motion Graphics templates in the Project panel, unlike media.

1. To add a template to the folder, just drag it or many into the Titles and Shapes panel. Another option is to use the install button on the bottom right of the screen to set up your MOGRTs.
2. You can open the Motion Graphics template by going to the folder where it is located. You can find the template in the Titles and Shapes panel when it has been added to the folder.

Note: A dialog box will show if there is already a Motion Graphics template with the same name. You will be asked to choose between overwriting the existing template or canceling the installation. When you attempt to install a Motion Graphics template, Premiere Elements will inform you if it is incompatible with your project version. If you use a later version of After Effects to create your motion graphics, the template will not work.

The Folder

Installation of MOGRTs or licensing of MOGRTs from Adobe Stock using the Titles & Shapes panel defaults to the Local Templates folder. You can find the folder at:

- macOS:username/Library/ApplicationSupport/Adobe/PremiereElements/25.0/Motion Graphics Templates/
- Windows: root://Users/username/AppData/Roaming/Adobe/Premiere Elements/25.0/ Motion Graphics Templates/

Note: The Applications folder in Windows and the Local Templates folder on macOS are not hidden. These files can be unhidden on your system if you want to see them.

Browse and manage Motion Graphics templates

The Titles and Shapes panel is where you can find Motion Graphics templates. Your Motion Graphics and free, expertly selected Stock templates can be seen and searched in the Titles and Shapes panel. **Here are some things you can do in the My Templates view:**

- To get precise results, use the search bar by entering a keyword.

- Templates with video thumbnails can have their animations seen with the help of a hover scrub.
- Organize the Motion Graphics templates in two ways: by Title and Recent Used.
- Select a Motion Graphics template and press the star button to make it your favorite. Then, use the Favorites filter near the search bar to view your favorites quickly.
- Rename and tag your Motion Graphics templates with the Info View for easier searching and organizing.

Use Motion Graphics templates from Adobe Stock

Images, transitions, titles, and lower thirds created by experts are available in Adobe Stock for use with Premiere Elements. The Titles and Shapes panel in Premiere Elements allows you to access Adobe Stock, where you can discover and personalize Motion Graphics layouts. Through Premiere Elements' Titles and Shapes panel, you can access Adobe Stock, where you can discover Motion Graphics designs.

Search Adobe Stock for Motion Graphics templates using the Titles and Shapes panel

The Titles and Shapes panel is where you can look for Motion Graphics templates in Adobe Stock.

1. Choose Adobe Stock on the Titles and Shapes panel's Templates tab.
2. Hit the Enter key after entering your search word.

Page results from Stocks are shown in Premiere Elements. If there are more things than can be displayed on the browser panel with a specific thumbnail slider size, then the number of pages will be determined by the total number of results. The number of pages varies about the size of the thumbnail slider or the view.

Here are several ways to get around the Stock results:

- By utilizing the previous and next arrows, you can navigate to the following or preceding page.
- Get to a certain page quickly by using the text edit field.
3. If you want to use the Motion Graphics template, you can either click the **License and Download (Free)** icon or drag it to the timeline.
4. Press the "**i**" symbol under a Motion Graphics template's thumbnail to see its details or get a preview of its animation.

You can also add the Motion Graphics template to your Local Templates folder by using the **License or Download (Free)** icon from this view.

Add Motion Graphic templates to the Timeline

1. Navigate to the **Titles and Shapes** panel, and then click the Templates tab to import a Motion Graphics template into the timeline.

2. You can select the template you want to use and drag it into a video track in your timeline.
3. When you add a template to the timeline, Premiere Elements shows the media as offline until the template completes loading. If the templates you added require fonts that have not been installed.

Note: There is more information to be found if the fonts needed by the templates you uploaded are not yet installed.

4. Once you've added a template to the timeline, you can change its look by going to the **Titles and Shapes** panel's **Edit tab**.

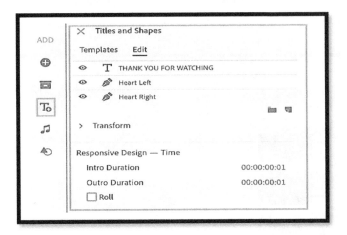

Customize your Motion Graphics template

To make changes to a template's properties, choose it in the timeline, then go to the **Titles and Shapes** panel, and finally, click **Edit**. **The options available to you in terms of Motion Graphics templates are:**

- Pick animation settings, color, and source text from the options provided by the template's author.
- Make changes to a wide variety of characteristics, including fonts, font size, faux styles, and more.
- If the After Effects author has created templates with:
  - Groups of controls: You can open and close your groups and use the properties within the group.
  - Replaceable media: You can replace images or videos with your own.

By modifying the controls, you can easily edit the template's properties. Choose the Motion Graphics template you want to edit in the timeline, and then use the red arrows on each side of the template to make it play longer or shorter.

Simplified timeline

Edit faster with a simplified Timeline

To make things easier to navigate, you can now see audio and video tracks grouped. The new Quick Tools menu makes it easy to access your frequently used editing tools. You can also lock individual tracks to avoid inadvertent modifications, among other features.

Add a clip to the timeline

Here are several methods to include clips in a sequence:

- To either the **Program Monitor** or the **Advanced View Timeline** panel, drag the clip from the **Project Assets** panel.
- You can add clips to the **Timeline** panel using the **Insert** and **Overwrite** buttons in the **Source Monitor's** contextual menu.
- In project assets, we can **right-click** > **Insert into Timeline**.

By erasing all frames in a sequence that begins at the edit point and continues throughout the clip, an overwrite edit inserts a new clip. When you drag a clip into a sequence or rearrange clips inside a series, the default technique is to overwrite. With an insert edit, if you want to put a clip into the sequence, you'll have to move any clips farther down the timeline to make room for it. To enter insert mode when dragging a clip, use Ctrl (Windows) or Command (macOS).

Align clips by using the Snap option

Aligning clips with each other or with certain moments in time is made easier using the **Snap** option, which is activated by default. When you use the Snap option, you can easily move clips around. Whether it's a marker, the beginning or end of the time ruler, the current time indication, or another clip, the clip will automatically line with its edge. To avoid accidentally inserting or overlaying elements when dragging, snapping is a great tool to have. An additional window will appear as you drag the clips, showing you the distance in frames that you have moved them. Assigning them to the beginning of the film is signified by a negative number.

1. Select **Timeline > Snap**. When an option is enabled, a check mark appears.

Drag video and audio to the Timeline

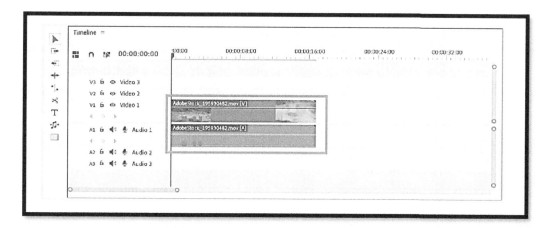

Unless the audio channel type of the clip is incompatible with the target track, when inserted into a sequence, the video and audio components of clips will show on appropriate tracks, for example, Video 1 and Audio 1. This causes the associated audio to play in the next available compatible track or triggers the automatic creation of a new suitable track. **Note:** Even if another audio clip is already playing on the incompatible track, dragging the audio clip to a different compatible track will cause it to move to the next available spot. So, be careful not to mess with the clips that are already there. To change this behavior, press and hold the Shift key while dragging. When you're adding a clip to a sequence, you can use the Program Monitor to see how it will look. The frames immediately surrounding the new clip's head and tail are seen during an overwrite edit. While inserting an alteration, it shows the frames right next to where you are inserting.

1. Using the Source Monitor, open a clip and mark its **In** and **Out points** (optional).

Note: Instead of going into the project assets panel and fiddling with the in and out points, you can just drag the clip or preview thumbnail there.

2. In a **Timeline** panel, make sure the **Snap** button is engaged to align clip borders as you move them.

3. **Pick one option out of these:**

   - You can easily separate a clip's audio and video segments by dragging and dropping it into a Timeline from the Source Monitor or Project panel. Hold down the Shift key until the video clip's segment appears above the selected video track. Keep your finger on the shift button and move the slider below the video/audio track separator. Let go of the mouse and Shift once the audio clip is above the track you want to listen to.

   - Paste the line that divides the video tracks from the audio tracks when dragging a clip from the Source Monitor or Project panel to the Video 1 track and any audio track for the audio. Place the clip above the audio track and drop it where you'd like the audio to land. While the audio section of the clip falls on the appropriate track, the visual portion stays in visual 1.

   - To initiate an overwrite edit, just move the clip from the Project or Source Monitor panel to the correct track in the Timeline panel where you would like it to begin. The region you want to overwrite is highlighted, and a pointer with the symbol appears.

   - You can introduce a clip into an existing project or Source Monitor by simply dragging it to the desired track in the Timeline panel at the desired starting point (Ctrl-drag on Windows, Command-drag on macOS). A pointer with the Insert icon appears, and the destination region is highlighted. At the insertion location, arrows show in all of the tracks.

   - From the Source Monitor or Project panel, you can insert, modify, and move tracks by dragging the clip to the desired track in the Timeline panel at the beginning of the desired track using **Ctrl+Alt-drag** (Windows) or **Command+Option-drag** (macOS). A pointer with the Insert icon appears, and the destination region is highlighted. The only tracks that display arrows at the insertion position are the ones to which the clip is added.

- If you're using a Roman keyboard, you can raise the zoom factor by dragging and pressing the equal sign key (=), or reduce it by using the negative sign key (-), when you drop a clip into a Timeline panel. The numeric keypad should not be utilized.

A Timeline panel will activate as the clip lands, allowing you to easily playback the newly added clip to the sequence.

Share via mobile app

To instantly share your precious moments with loved ones on any social media platform or messaging app, you can use the Adobe Elements (Beta) mobile app to scan a QR code. You can use this function to produce a QR code and share media straight from the Elements organizer desktop program. Just choose one or more media files, and then choose the 'Share via Mobile app' option from the 'Share' dropdown.

1. To access other sharing options, choose the media in Elements Organizer and then click the **Share** button.

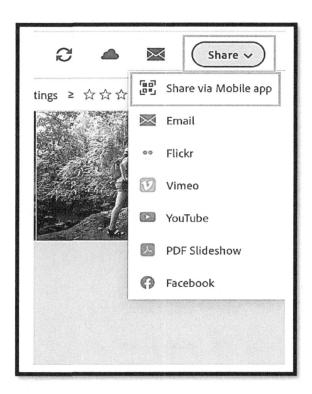

2. Please choose the option; **Share via Mobile app**. Your chosen media will begin to be uploaded to your Adobe cloud storage account.

Note: If your media is already on the Adobe cloud, it will not be uploaded again. Your Adobe account comes with 2GB of free cloud storage.

3. After you upload the media you've chosen to the cloud, a QR code will be automatically produced.

4. Use the camera on your mobile device to scan this QR code. The Adobe Elements (Beta) app for mobile devices will launch when you tap this.
5. Select the sharing center in the mobile app to distribute your media to any location you desire.

Note: The QR code serves as a link to the App Store, where you can download the program if it is not already installed. Kindly use your mobile device's camera to scan the QR code once again after installing the app.

Setting Up Your First Project

Creating a New Project

1. **Open Adobe Premiere Elements**: Turn on your computer and launch Adobe Premiere Elements. If you haven't done so before, visit the Adobe website and install the most recent version.
2. **Welcome Screen**: When you first launch the program, you will often see the Welcome screen. In such a case, find it in the menu by selecting **"File"** followed by **"New Project."**
3. **New Project Setup:**

Name of the Project: Use this space to give your project a name. Picking a name that conveys the nature of the project is important.

Location: Make your selection for the location to save your project files under **"Save to."** To get to the place you want, click the **"Browse"** button.

Video Presets: Use the presets to get the perfect video configuration for your project. Among other things, this configuration determines the video's size and frame rate.

Editing style: Determine which style is most appropriate for your project. Imagine for a moment that you are making a standard video. Make your selection between "**Full HD 1080i**" and "**Full HD 1080p**."

Timebase: Set the timebase for your project. Most projects can get by with the default option.

4. **Organize and Edit**: To begin working on a new project once you've finished organizing and editing it, click the "**OK**" button. After then, Adobe Premiere Elements' editing interface will pop up. You are now ready to begin editing your video, adding media, and organizing your clips.

5. **Timeline**: The media you downloaded can be easily added to the timeline to begin editing and constructing your film. You'll assemble your clips, modify the timeline, and apply effects, transitions, and more.

6. **Save Your Project**: Remember to save your project regularly if you want to keep your work. To accomplish this, go to the "**File**" menu and select "**Save**" or "**Save As.**"

Open a project

Adobe Premiere Elements only allows you to have one active project at a time, so keep that in mind. To effectively launch an existing project, you must have both the project file (**.PREL**) and the associated code files on your computer.

Adobe Premiere Elements offers many ways to access previously saved projects:

1. **On the home screen:**

Launch Adobe Premiere Elements. Either go to the "**Recent Files**" list or select "**Video Editor**" from the Home screen to open the project you desire. To launch Premiere Elements, choose "**Video Editor**" if the file you wish to open isn't already in the list of recently used files. In Premiere Elements, locate the project file you wish to open by going to the "**File**" menu and selecting "**Open Project**." Continue by clicking on the file.

2. **If Premiere Elements Is Already Open:**

If Adobe Premiere Elements is already open, go to the "**File**" menu. Go to the drop-down menu and select "**Open Project**" or "**Open Recent Project**." Select the project file you wish to open by pointing to it with the cursor and clicking "**Open**."

3. **Right from Windows's File Explorer:**

Locate the folder on your hard drive that contains the "**.PREL**" project file. Make two clicks on the project file. Doing so should trigger Adobe Premiere Elements to launch the selected project right away.

Customizing the Workspace

To keep all of the panels within the given program window, Premiere Elements employs a docking technique. In contrast, panels are flexible in size and placement, giving you the freedom to create a work environment that suits your needs. There are substantial dividing lines that run vertically and horizontally between the Monitor, Tasks, and My Project panels while you have Premiere Elements open. Any time you need additional room to work in one of the panels, you can just move these dividers to make that happen.

1. To make the two-headed cursor appear, you need to position your pointer across the line that divides the **My Project** and **Monitor panels**. Then, to make the **My Project panel** taller, pull it up toward the Monitor panel.

To make the Monitor panel bigger, just slide it to the right. Similarly, to make the Tasks panel longer, just drag it to the left. You can choose from the two options.

2. The **Restore Workspace** option allows you to put the panels back in their original order and can be accessed from the **Window menu**. Keep in mind that once moved, everything goes back to its original spot. When you notice that your screen is getting too busy, it might be time to rearrange your workplace.

The panel docking headers can be hidden by default in Premiere Elements. To make better use of the real estate on your screen, they've hidden the headers that normally display the title, panel menu, and close buttons.

3. You can see the docking headers if you go to **Window > Show Docking Headers**. Select **Window > Hide Docking Headers** to hide them again.

Even though each panel is docked into a specific spot in the conventional workspace design, there are situations where a more flexible setting could be more beneficial. All you have to do is **undock**, or "**float**," your panels to do this.

4. If the docking headers are not visible, you can make them visible by going to **Window > Show Docking Headers.** The next step is to click the **My Project panel's docking header**, and then drag it slightly in the direction you choose. The panel will become translucent as you drag the header. As soon as you release the mouse button, the My Project panel will appear as a floating window. Because of this, the Tasks panel and the Monitor panel can splay out toward the main window's base.

5. By pressing the red Close button (⬤) located in the upper-left corner of the My Project panel, you may finally close the panel.

One hint for multi-monitor setups is to use the main monitor to display the program window and the secondary monitor to display any floating windows you may want.

6. From the Window menu, select **Window > My Project** to reopen the panel. Remember that the panel opens exactly where you left it last time. This is because Premiere Elements retains the panel positions as an element of the editable workspace and recalls them when necessary.

7. Select **Window > Restore Workspace** to return the workspace to its initial condition.

CHAPTER 2

GETTING STARTED WITH VIDEO EDITING

Introduction to Video Editing and Adobe Premiere Elements

To make a final product that tells a narrative or delivers a message, video editing involves modifying and organizing video media. To make anything visually appealing and relevant, it is necessary to trim, combine, and improve footage while adding effects, transitions, and audio components. Video editing is a talent that is vital in today's digital age, whether for personal projects, social media, or professional material. The technical expertise sometimes demanded by sophisticated software makes the prospect of video editing seem daunting to amateurs and newcomers. Adobe Premiere Elements is useful in this situation. If you want to start editing videos but are intimidated by the steep learning curve of professional products like Adobe Premiere Pro, Adobe Premiere Elements is a great option since it simplifies the process and makes it fun. When compared to other editing tools, Premiere Elements stands out because it satisfies both advanced users and those just starting. It comes with a ton of features that let you be creative while making professional-looking films. An easy-to-navigate interface walks users through each stage of the editing process, and the program provides many settings to accommodate users of varying abilities. For example, individuals who want to work quickly can switch to Quick mode, while those who are more comfortable with thorough editing will find more options in Advanced mode.

Guided Edits is a tool that many users love in Premiere Elements. Users may apply effects, and transitions, or make precise modifications with the aid of these in-app, interactive lessons rather than searching for external instructions. Those just starting in the field of editing, or anybody else who wants to hone their abilities without the hassle of guessing will find this hands-on method very helpful. You may also take advantage of the software's automated features, such as Auto Creations, which can make video collages and slideshows for you. What this implies for users is that they may build their films from the ground up to reflect their vision. For instance, Smart Trim may utilize AI to find the most visually appealing segments in your movie and use them, saving you time and work. A variety of transitions and effects are available in Premiere Elements, allowing users to give their films a more polished appearance. Improving a project using filters, slow-motion effects, and animated overlays doesn't require a lot of technical knowledge. It also includes easy-to-use audio tools, so users may improve the experience by adding voiceovers, sound effects, and background music. When dealing with several footage and audio files, the organization becomes even more important in video editing. An Organizer feature is built into Premiere Elements to assist users in efficiently managing their material.

Using this function streamlines the entire process by making it easier to locate, categorize, and tag movies and photographs. With Premiere Elements, distributing your finished film is a breeze. The program has simple export choices that allow you to share the video on social media or save it in a format that is compatible with a wide range of devices. If you want to share your work online or just keep it for yourself, this is a great tool for you. In conclusion, Adobe Premiere Elements video editing allows for freedom of expression without the burden of learning complex tools. Even inexperienced users may create professional-looking films with its well-rounded set of tools and capabilities. Video editing has never been easier than with Premiere Elements, whether you're making content for social media, editing home videos, or trying out new ideas.

Importing Media Files: Photos, Videos, and Audio

Import in bulk

   1. **Go to the Organizer workspace:**

Launch Adobe Premiere Elements and locate the "**Organizer**" area.

   2. **Start importing in bulk:**

In the Organizer area, select the "**Import**" option. Next, choose "**In Bulk."**

   3. **Pick out the source folder:**

Locate the folder on your computer that has subfolders containing your media files, and then choose them when the "**Import Media**" window appears. If the folder containing the media files you wish to import is not already displayed, you can access it by clicking "**Add Folder**" and then navigating through your computer's directories.

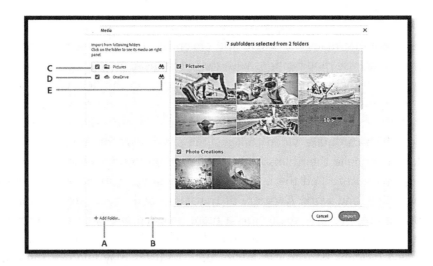

A. Add a folder **B.** Remove the selected folder **C.** Select a folder **D.** Import from OneDrive (Windows only) **E.** Watch a folder

4. Pick which subfolders to import:

On the right side of the **Import Media** dialog box, you can see all the subfolders that are inside the main folder you selected. Locate the folders containing the media files you wish to import into Adobe Premiere Elements, and then choose them. Choose all subfolders or select only the ones you need, depending on your requirements.

Import from camera or card reader

You can easily import your media files from your camera or card reader into Elements Organizer.

1. Connect your camera or card reader:

Remember to use the correct cable or card adapter when connecting your camera or card reader to your computer.

2. Go to the Organizer workspace:

Access the Organizer workspace in Adobe Premiere Elements.

3. Start importing from a camera or card reader:

Select "**Import**" from the Organizer menu, and then choose "**From Camera or Card Reader.**"

4. Set up the import settings:

Select the location from which you would like to import the images or videos using the "**Get Photos From**" drop-down menu located on the "**Source**" tab of the **Photo Downloader** dialog box.

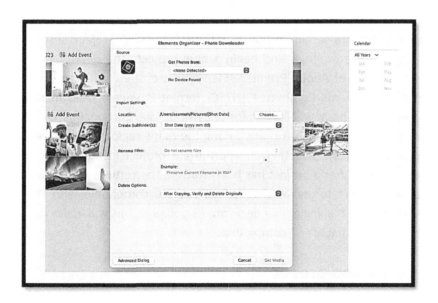

Use the defaults or tweak the "**Import Settings**" to make the import process work for you.

5. Start importing media:

You can begin the import process by clicking "**Get Media**" when you have finished configuring the options.

6. Handle Attached Keyword Tags (if asked):

Select the Keyword Tags you wish to import with the media files in the "**Import Attached Keyword Tags**" box. Select the desired **Keyword Tags** and hit "**OK**." With any luck, a notification reading "**Files Successfully Copied**" will appear after the transfer is complete. To complete the import, click "**OK**" to indicate your understanding.

Understanding Project Settings

The project parameters in Adobe Premiere Elements dictate the program's behavior towards the media files you load. The overall functionality of your project is impacted by these options, which encompass aspects such as format, source, aspect ratio, frame rate, audio sample rate, field order, and bit level. If you have an AVCHD video file and want to know where it originated from—a hard drive or a Flash memory camera, for instance—you may find that information in the project settings. In addition to allowing you to select between standard and widescreen video formats, the project options also determine the aspect ratio. Additionally, these settings provide crucial technical details, such as the frame rate (the number of displayed frames per second), the audio sample rate (the quality of the sound), and whether the video uses the upper or lower field first (which affects how it plays and compatibility with various display systems). A pixel's bit depth determines how much color information it can hold. Both the depth of the project and the accuracy of the colors are affected by this.

These preferences are pre-set in Adobe Premiere Elements' project setup, which is used whenever you launch the program and begin a new project. The default TV standard project settings in most versions of Adobe Premiere Elements are often sufficient for most users. The National Television Standards Committee (NTSC) format is widely used in the Americas, the Caribbean, Japan, South Korea, and Taiwan for television. Asia, Europe, Russia, Africa, the Middle East, India, Australia, and New Zealand are among the many regions that make extensive use of PAL (Phase Alternating Line). Selecting an appropriate project location for the genre of your source picture is crucial. After a project has been started, the settings cannot be changed. Verify that your source footage's format and specifications are compatible with the project preset you're considering before making a final decision. As you edit, this will assist you stay away from issues caused by settings that aren't compatible.

Dynamic sequence preset

Adobe Premiere Elements adapts the project settings behind the scenes so they fit the characteristics of the video clip you add to the timeline in the Advanced view. Size, frame rate, field order, and pixel aspect ratio are a few of them.

Select presets and change settings

That's why Adobe Premiere Elements has several default project settings tailored to common media types like cameras, DVDs, and mobile phones. With these presets, you may quickly and easily create projects by accessing pre-configured options for common media types. There are several presets available in Adobe Premiere Elements when a new project is being started. It should be mentioned that users are not allowed to create their templates. Potential themes are defined by the choices that were accessible when the project was initiated. Once a project has been created, it is not possible to alter its settings. Users may readily find the Project Presets in the New Project text box, allowing them to choose the best option for their media source. Presets are preconfigured versions of these that include crucial parameters including format, aspect ratio, frame rate, recording parameters, and more. Clicking the "**More**" button in the New Project window box will bring you a list of all the themes along with their options. At this point, you can see a complete catalog of all the presets and a short description of their settings by clicking the "**View All Presets**" button.

Select a project preset

1. **Open Adobe Premiere Elements**: Launch Adobe Premiere Elements on your PC.
2. **Access the Home Screen**. A new project can be started by navigating to "**File**" > "**New**" > "**Project**," or by clicking on "**Video Editor**" on the Home Screen.
3. **Pick a Preset**: Various presets are available in the "**New Project**" box; they are categorized as "**Landscape**," "**Portrait**," "**Square**," or "**Social**." Just choose one!

You can browse more presets categorized by **Video Standard** and **Aspect Ratio** by choosing "**More**" and then "**View All Presets**."

4. **Choose the Right Preset**: Look over the available presets and select the one that is most compatible with the video's format, TV standard, or aspect ratio; this will help you choose the right one to edit.

Verify that the specifications and features of your media source are compatible with the configuration you selected.

5. **Confirm and Proceed**: After you've discovered the optimal option for your film, click "**OK**" to confirm your selection and go forward.
6. **Name and Save Your Project**: A dialogue box will appear, asking you to give your project a name and choose a location to save it.

Choose a safe location to store your project and give it a meaningful name. Following that, choose the desired settings for the project and click "**OK**" to proceed.

Change settings for an existing project

You are limited to making specific adjustments to a project's parameters in Adobe Premiere Elements once it has been created. Specifically, after the project has been made, you will not be able to alter the primary preferences for Editing mode or the style of Preview files. Nonetheless, there is still time to make minor adjustments to the program. **Here are the ways to access and modify specific project parameters in Adobe Premiere Elements:**

1. **Go to the project settings:**

Open Adobe Premiere Elements and open your project.

2. **Go to the Project Settings page:**

Press "**Edit**" on the menu bar. Pick "**Project Settings**" from the corresponding drop-down menu, and then go to "**General**."

3. **Choose the project settings:**

There are options to change settings for General, Capture, and Video Rendering in the Project Settings text box that comes up. Change or modify the settings in this text box as needed to meet your needs. Be aware that after you've established a project, you won't be able to modify critical parameters like Editing mode or the Preview file type, but you can make minor adjustments to the display and other settings.

4. **Make the Changes:**

When you've finished adjusting the settings as needed, click "**OK**" to save your changes. Bear in mind that essential preferences, such as editing mode and preview file format, cannot be changed once a project has been created in Adobe Premiere Elements. In the Project Settings dialog box, you can make minor adjustments to display-related settings. Before you begin building the project, double-check that these crucial settings are suitable for your requirements.

Check your project settings

In the project presets, you'll find three categories of settings: **General, Capture, and Video Rendering**. You can't modify most of the options after a project has started, including frame rate, size, and aspect ratio. To be sure the media you wish to add is compatible with the project, you can check the options.

- First, open the project in Premiere Elements. Then, go to **Edit > Project Settings > [category].**

Editing in Quick View and Guided

By providing a framework, the Quick view timeline allows you to easily arrange your clips into a movie. It shows every video as a series of frames that span the whole length of the clip. To view the entire video, simply drag the bar to the right. By dragging the leftmost slider to the left, you can magnify the video and observe its details more closely. **On the Quick view timeline, you can find the following tracks:**

- **Title:** Give your video clip a name and give it a title on this track.
- **Video:** To edit your video, use this track.
- **Sound:** Insert any necessary background music and other sounds here.

- **Narration:** Include a voiceover for your video under this track's narration options.

Use the Quick view timeline to quickly put together a movie using your clips. You need to click the scissors icon on the time indicator to cut a clip and remove an unwanted part. Utilizing the panels situated in the Action bar—found at the screen's base—you can incorporate music, titles, transitions, and special effects into your movie.

Adding clips in the Quick View timeline

To add clips from the Finder to the Quick view timeline, just drag & drop them. The Quick View timeline also has an Add Media window that you may use to import clips from many different sources. Once you've uploaded all of your videos, you may easily reorder them in the timeline of Quick view. A clip can be added to the beginning or conclusion of a series, or even divided before being added.

Insert a clip into the timeline for the Quick view

Here are the steps:

1. To add a clip to the Quick view timeline, just drag it from the Finder. A green vertical line will show you the drop zone when you slide the clip across the timeline in Quick view. Here is where you may attach the clip. When the insert icon shows up and the pointer goes to that spot, you can release the mouse button.
2. Using the arrow keys, transfer the video clip from the Finder to the Monitor panel. Upon import, the clip will be automatically put into the Quick view timeline.

Add a clip in the Quick view timeline by inserting one clip before another

1. Pick out a clip from Finder and drop it onto the timeline of the Quick view to utilize it.
2. Any subsequent clips will be shifted to the right, and the one you dropped it on will be superimposed over the freshly inserted one.

Add one clip after another in the Quick view timeline

1. Select the clip that will appear before the one you wish to add the new clip to in the Quick view timeline.
2. Use the drag-and-drop feature to transfer the clip from the Finder to the Monitor panel or the Quick view timeline.
3. As more clips are added, they will also be displayed to the right of the selected clip.

Move a clip in the Quick View timeline

Here are the steps:

1. Simply drag the desired clip from its present position in the Quick view timeline to a new one, either before or after the one you wish to relocate. Once the insert icon is displayed, position the clip in the drop zone, denoted by a vertical green line.
2. Release the mouse button.
3. As with all subsequent clips, this one moves to the right after relocation.

Copy and paste clips in the Quick View timeline

You can change their sequence of appearance simply by copying and pasting video clips into your project. To insert clips between existing clips or to overlay them on top of frames that are already there, you can copy and paste multiple clips at once. All the clips are maintained at the same relative timing. When the current time indicator appears in Adobe Premiere Elements 11, clips are placed into the Video 1 or Audio 1 track. On the other hand, it can skip this step if you manually transfer clips over several tracks. In the Quick view timeline, when you insert a clip, the current-time indicator will jump to the very end of the clip. It becomes easy to conduct successive paste operations.

Here are the steps:

1. Use the Quick view timeline to choose several movie clips and arrange them. Selecting only the audio or video portion of linked clips is as easy as alt-clicking the selected clip.
2. **Copy** can be accessed in the **Edit** menu.
3. To start pasting in Quick view, drag the current time indicator to the beginning of the clip, and then select an option:
   o To replace or overlay the current video on the track with new content, choose **Edit > Paste.**
   o To paste the copied clips and relocate any existing information, go to the menu bar and select **Edit > Paste Insert.**

Always keep in mind that you can copy and paste the properties of a clip, including its opacity, loudness, motion, and other effects, into another clip.

Zoom in or out of the Quick View timeline

Zooming in on the timeline in Quick view enlarges the region around the current time indicator. You can examine smaller and more detailed parts of the video in this way. If you want to focus on the region around the cursor instead of the time indicator, you may use the zoom feature while making a clip. Before you let go of the mouse, you can see exactly where the insertion point is with this technique. However, the Quick view timeline becomes increasingly visible as you increase the zoom level, giving you a more in-depth visual summary of the film.

Here are the steps:

1. Select an option from the following on the Quick view timeline:
   - You can adjust the clip's size in the Quick view timeline when you drag it to zoom in or out. To increase the zoom factor, use the **Equals (=)** key while holding down the left mouse button. Instead, press the **Minus (-)** key to decrease the zoom factor.
   - You can adjust the zoom level when adding clips by dragging them to the Quick view timeline. Hold down the left mouse button and press the semicolon (;) key to increase the zoom factor. The negative sign (-) key is used to decrease the level of zoom.
   - To zoom in on the Quick view timeline, either click the Zoom In button or drag the Zoom slider to the right.
   - You can close the Quick view timeline by clicking the Zoom Out button or dragging the Zoom slider to the left.

You can go back to the previous zoom level or watch the whole video in the Quick View timeline by clicking the "**Fit To Visible Timeline**" button. Alternatively, you can use the **Backslash (\)** key to do the same task. Make sure the Quick view timeline is activated before pressing the **Backslash (\)** key. Also, instead of using the numeric keypad, you can use the **Equals (=)** or **Minus (-)** keys on your keyboard to zoom in or out of the image. Press the **Yen symbol key** to see the whole movie in the Quick view timeline. Pressing this will enlarge the timeline, allowing you to view the full movie. You must activate the Quick View timeline before pressing the **Yen symbol key.**

Delete a clip in the Quick View timeline

Here are the steps:

1. The Quick view displays a timeline; select a clip from there.
2. Use the Control key to right-click the clip, and then select an option:
   - **Delete and close the gap**

Deletes the clip and then moves other clips to fill the space in their timelines.
   - **Remove audio**

The audio from your movie will not be played.

Working with the Advanced Views

Your film project is shown graphically in the Advanced View of the timeline as vertically stacked video and audio segments in tracks. The individual clips will appear in the sequence they were captured when you capture video from a digital video device. A time ruler is employed in the Expert timeline view to depict the many elements of your film and their interconnections as they unfold over time. You can edit and construct sequences, add transitions, identify important frames, and control the arrangement of clips. Using the controls on the Advanced View timeline, you may pan the camera around to see the whole film, or you can zoom in to explore individual scenes in greater depth. You also have the opportunity to resize the tracks and the header area, change the way clips display in the tracks, and more.

Tracks in the Advanced View timeline

By utilizing tracks, one may incorporate many elements like as compositing effects, picture-in-picture effects, overlay titles, soundtracks, and audio or video layers. With several audio tracks, you can use one to add background music and another to narrate. Each video and audio file is now an integral part of the finished film. Typically, there are three tracks on the timeline in Advanced View: one for audio and video, one for narration, and one for sound. By dragging and dropping, you may join linked clips—video and audio clips that are connected—to a track. The video and audio parts of a linked clip (e.g., Video1 and Audio1) show up on the same track, with the video part directly above the audio. For the Advanced View timeline to display all the songs, you might have to scroll up or down a bit. To add a new video track to the project, just drag and drop a clip into the active video track. There is no restriction on how many songs may be part of a project. Even before you submit footage, you have the freedom to add or remove songs whenever you choose. The track might be empty, but movies must feature at least one genre from each of its sections. The order in which the video tracks are played is extremely important since any clip discovered in Video 2 will also overrun the Video 1 track. The order of the tracks is irrelevant because the recordings are combined when the audio is played back. You have the option to specify the default number of tracks and the kind of tracks for new movies, which is certainly beneficial.

Advanced View timeline tools

At the very top of the timeline in Advanced View are the controls you need to play, stop, and adjust the pace of a clip. The panels in the Action bar also allow you to add music, titles, transitions, and special effects. Additionally, you may add narration, locate musical beats, launch the Audio Mixer, and add markers.

Move through the Advanced View timeline

Before you continue to place and rearrange clips in the Advanced View timeline, make sure the current-time indicator is in the appropriate spot. The current time indication in the time ruler is correlated with the frame that is presently presented in the Monitor panel. An elongated vertical line that passes through all of the tracks indicates the current time. By adjusting the magnification level of the Advanced View timeline, you can precisely locate the spot on the timeline where you wish to insert a clip or apply an edit.

Choose an option from the following on the Advanced View timeline:

- You can adjust the displayed time by dragging the indicator.
- Select the area on the time ruler where you would want to have the current time displayed, and then click on it.
- To fixate the current time indication to the closest clip or marker, drag it while pressing and holding the **Shift** key.
- To alter the time value, move the time display beneath the Monitor panel.
- To modify the time, go to the bottom of the Monitor panel and find the time display. After that, type in the right time and press the **Enter** key. (Adobe Premiere Elements treats values below 100 as frames, but you don't have to provide leading zeroes, colons, or semicolons.)

Note: If you want to jump between the beginning of the video and the finish, you may do so by pressing the **Home or End keys** on your computer. By utilizing the **Page Up and Page Down keys** on your keyboard, you can navigate the current-time indication to the prior or subsequent clip. The time indication will go forward one frame when you hit the **Right Arrow key,** and back one frame when you use the **Left Arrow key**. You can forward or rewind the current time indicator by five frames at a time by pressing the **Shift** key with the **Right or Left Arrow key.**

Add clips to the Advanced View timeline

In the Advanced View, when you enter a clip into the timeline, the clips on all tracks that are directly next to it will relocate to create room for it. There is no loss of sync between the audio and video of previously recorded clips when all of them are relocated simultaneously. In some cases, it may not be desirable for all of the clips to be moved with each insert. If you're adding music to the backdrop that will play across the entire video, for example, you probably don't want the clips to animate. You can move clips together when you insert them by using the Alt key. You can only use a maximum of two tracks at once to transfer individual clips. There are two tracks involved in this process: the one being added and the one containing the audio or video (if any). The aligned and synchronized tracks travel in tandem with one another. The other songs' footage remained unaffected.

Insert a clip, and then move clips along the timeline in the Advanced View

Choose an option from the following and act accordingly:

- You can drag the clip from the **Project Assets** panel to the area you want it to be in the **Advanced View** timeline. You can release your grip on the mouse after the Insert icon has shown and the pointer has shifted to that spot.

- To change the location of the current time indication on the **Advanced View** timeline, drag it to the desired spot. Next, choose the desired clip from the Project Assets tab and then click **Clip > Insert.**

Insert a clip, shift clips on only the target and linked tracks

While holding down the **Alt** key, drag the clip from the Project Assets panel to the correct spot on the **Advanced View** timeline. Release the mouse button after the Insert icon is visible and the pointer has moved to the desired spot. If you drag the clip you wish to edit into an empty place above the top video track (for video) or below the bottom audio track (for audio), Adobe Premiere Elements will create a new track for the clip. A new video track and an audio track will be created if the clip contains both types of media.

Overlay a clip in the Advanced View timeline

The fastest and easiest way to replace a portion of a video is to layer one piece of footage over another. The new clip you add when you overlay it will replace all frames before the one you chose in the timeline. The new clip will span the whole 40-frame duration of the old one. If any frames follow the overlay, they maintain their previous place on the track. Unless the extra material supplied by the overlay carries over after the original film ends, overlays do not change the running time of the film.

Pick an action from the list:
- Hold down the **Control key** or the **Command key** and drag the clip from the **Project Assets panel** to the first frame you wish to overlay. You are free to release the mouse button after the overlay icon appears at the location of the pointer.
- After dragging the current time indication to the desired starting frame for the overlay, choose the desired clip in the **Project Assets** panel, and then, from the drop-down menu, pick **Clip > Overlay.**

Place one clip above another in the Advanced View timeline

In contrast to overlays, you can stack clips without removing any footage from the clip below it. For example, several keying effects can be applied to such stacked clips.

Here are the steps:
1. Locate the video clip you want to overlay on top of the current one in the Advanced View timeline, and then drag the current time indicator to that spot.
2. Press and hold the **shift** key while you drag a clip from the Project Assets panel to the Monitor panel.
3. Choose the **Place On Top** option.

Adobe Premiere Elements moves the second clip to the first available video track, right next to the time indicator, after importing it into the project.

Replace a clip in the Advanced View timeline

In Advanced View, you can use the **Replace Clip command** to swap out a clip during the timeline without affecting its length, effects, or overlays. You will discover this option to be useful when modifying bigger instant films.

Here are the steps:

1. Select the video clip you wish to incorporate into your project from the **Project Assets panel.**

2. To replace a clip in the timeline, go to the **Advanced View** and right-click or control-click on it. Then, select **Replace Clip from Project Assets** from the option that shows. The length of the entering clip is compared to the outgoing clip's length; if the incoming clip is longer, its end is chopped.

You will be prompted to either stop the process of replacing the clip or utilize black frames to fill in the leftover time if the incoming clip is shorter than the one being replaced.

Select, move, align, and delete clips in the Advanced View timeline

You can discover that you need to reposition clips, cut and paste scenes, or delete clips after adding them to your video. There are some ways to choose clips, including individual ones, groups of clips, or even only the audio or video portion of a linked clip.

Select clips in the Advanced View timeline

With the click of a mouse, you can do any of the following actions:

- In the Advanced View timeline, click on the clip you wish to pick to choose it individually. If many clips are linked or grouped, choosing one will likewise choose all of them.

- Holding down the **Alt** key while clicking on the desired clip allows you to choose only the audio or video portion of linked clips.

- Hold down the **Alt** key while clicking the clip you wish to pick to choose it from inside a group.

- Click on each clip you want to select and hold down the **Shift** key to select multiple clips at once. (To deselect a clip, click on it again while holding **Shift**.)

- Marked selection is drawing a rectangle that includes the clips you wish to choose in order. By doing so, the clips will be chosen consecutively.

- To add clips to the current selection, draw a marquee around them while holding **Shift**. By doing so, the clips will be added to the selection.

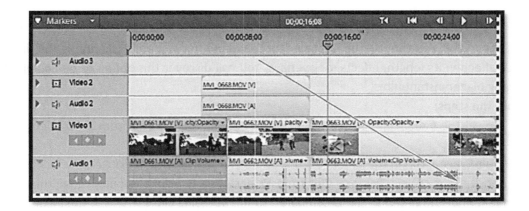

Move a clip in the Advanced View timeline

The Advanced View timeline allows you to easily reorder clips by dragging and dropping them. **You can use the same steps to insert or overlay clips as you move them; just follow the steps to add clips.**

- All of the tracks will move after you drag a clip to the new location where you want it to be put. You are free to release the mouse button after the Insert icon has shown and been selected.
- Press the **Control or Command key** combination after dragging the clip you wish to include in the video to the first frame you wish to superimpose. With this, you can reposition the clip and add it to another scene in the film. You are free to release the mouse button after the overlay icon appears at the location of the pointer.
- Hold down the **Alt** key while selecting the clip you wish to move to move only one of two linked clips simultaneously. Move it to where you want it by dragging it. When the cursor changes to the Insert icon, release the mouse button if you want to move clips just on the target tracks. You can now selectively move clips on such tracks. To add another clip as an overlay, press **Ctrl**, and then release the mouse button when the **Overlay icon** appears.

Align clips by using the Snap option

With the **Snap** option enabled by default, it is considerably easier to match clips with each other or with certain times in the past. Relocating a clip is feasible when you use the Snap option. A marker, the beginning and ending points of the time ruler, the current time indicator, or another clip's edge will cause the clip to automatically align itself. To avoid inadvertently making an insert or overlay change while dragging, snapping is a good idea. The reason for this is that when you snap, you won't align neighboring items by accident. A window will appear whenever you drag and drop a clip; it will display the exact distance in frames that the clip has been moved. When you insert them further into the film than they originally were, a negative number signifies that.

1. Go to **Timeline > Snap**. You can utilize the option if a checkmark appears next to it.

Remove/Delete a clip from the timeline using either the Quick view or the Advanced View

A scene cut from a film will not affect the final cut in any way. The clip can still be viewed through the Project Assets tab.

1. In the timeline, choose a clip or clips in the Quick view or the Advanced View. (To pick only a clip's audio or video, press the **Alt** key on your keyboard.)
2. **Do anything from the list of possible things:**
   o To delete clips and create a space of the same length, select "**Edit > Delete**" from the menu bar. This action is called "**clearing**."
   o Choose **Edit > Delete And Close Gap** from the menu bar or press the **Delete or Backspace key** on your keyboard to delete a clip and close the gap that is left behind, often known as a ripple deletion.

Keep in mind that the transition that was meant to follow a deleted clip will also be erased from the Quick view timeline. When you delete a clip from the timeline in Advanced View, it also deletes the clip that came before it and the clip that came after it in the transition chain.

Delete space between clips in the Advanced View timeline

You can quickly eliminate any gap between clips by using the **Delete and Close Gap** tool in the Advanced view timeline. The **Delete** and **Backspace** keys could be another option to explore. To bridge the gap, both strategies entail repositioning clips that are nearby.

1. Select an option from the following in the Advanced view timeline:
   o Click the space's context menu once again after selecting **Erase and Close Gap** from there.
   o To begin, find the area with unwanted text and click on it. Then, use the **Delete or Backspace key.**

To make things easier, you can drag the current time indicator to the gap and then click the **Zoom In button** if the gap is really small and hard to choose.

Create a duplicate clip in the Advanced View timeline

From the Project Assets panel, drag a source clip into the Advanced View timeline to create a clip instance. The clip instance will be generated as a result of this. By default, this instance starts and ends at the same places as the original clip. All instances of the clip seen in the Advanced View timeline will likewise be deleted if you delete the original clip in the Project Assets panel. Making a copy of the original clip in the Project Assets tab will let you make new clips with different starting and ending positions. When you remove a clip from the Project Assets panel, it will also remove all instances of it from the Advanced View timeline.

1. In the Project Assets panel, choose a clip you like. Then, go to the menu bar and choose **Edit > Duplicate.**
2. Go to the **Project Assets** tab, select the duplicate clip, and rename it as you like by:
   o Selecting "**Rename**" from the Clip menu, then provide a new name.
   o Clicking the text and begin typing to change your name.

To duplicate an existing clip in the Project Assets panel, you can either copy and paste it or drag and drop it while holding down the **Control** key.

View the duration of selected clips in the Advanced View timeline

In the Info panel, you can see how long it will take for various clips that you've selected in the timeline's Quick view or Advanced View to replay. It would be good to have this information when editing a movie. For instance, you may want to select scenario-specific music or swap out some samples for something else entirely. The Information panel will display the total duration for all of the clips you've selected in the Project Assets panel as you make your selections. The length of the selected clips is shown in the Information panel, which updates as you move the mouse over them in the Quick view or Advanced View timelines. By starting the computation from the In point of the first clip that was chosen and continuing until the Out point of the final clip that was chosen, the length may be estimated. If the clips aren't sequential in the tracks, the total duration of the tracks can be more than the sum of their clip times.

1. Make sure the player can view the Info panel. In case it isn't visible, go to **Window > Info.**
2. In either the Advanced View timeline, the Quick view timeline, or the Project Assets panel, choose the relevant clips. In the Info panel, you can see the total time for all of the selected objects as well as their total number of selections.

Note: The duration of a clip may be found by placing the cursor over it in either the Quick view or the Advanced View timeline. A tooltip will then display this information.

Customize Advanced View timeline tracks

To better suit your project's needs, you can adjust the timeline tracks in the Advanced View.

Add a track to the Advanced View timeline

Here are the steps:
1. Choose the **Timeline** menu and go to **Add Tracks.**
2. Enter the desired track count in the **Add area** of the **Add Tracks dialog** box, which can be found in either the video or audio track section.

3. For each type of track you've uploaded, a pop-up menu labeled "**Placement**" will appear; select an option and then click **OK**. You can use this to find out where the songs will go.

Resize tracks

Three distinct sizes are set for tracks: small, medium, and large. To see thumbnails of clips and adjust effects like opacity and volume, the Big view is a lifesaver. You can also browse the thumbnails of the clips in this format. You can also change the width of the space that shows track headers and manually resize tracks if you need to accommodate longer track names. If your film has many tracks, you can adjust their proportional distribution to give more prominence to the ones you like. The names of tracks are hidden by default. To view the track names, you need to make the track header section larger.

Resize the height of a track

1. In the timeline for the Advanced View, pick one of the following options:
   ○ Choose "**Track Size**" from the context menu that appears when you right-click or control-click an empty track in the Advanced View timeline. Next pick either the Small, the Medium, or the Large option.
   ○ On the Advanced View timeline, position the cursor between two tracks in the track header section. This will trigger the Height Adjustment icon to show. Next, use the up and down arrows on your mouse to resize the track above (for audio) or the track below (for video) (for audio).

Resize the track header section of the Advanced View timeline

1. Position the pointer above the right edge of the track header (the region where the track icons are shown) in the Advanced View of the timeline. The Resize icon will then appear. When you're done, drag the edge to the right. You can tell the track header is at least a certain width by looking at the symbols up above. The widest point is almost twice as broad as the narrowest point.

Rename a track

1. In the timeline's Advanced View, right-click or control-click the name of the track (for example, Video 1), and then choose the **Rename option**.
2. Change the track's name by clicking outside the box or by continuing to type the name and pressing **Enter**.

Delete empty tracks from the Advanced View timeline

1. **Pick an action from the list:**
   o   Go to the Timeline menu and choose **Delete Empty Tracks**.
   o   Select the **Delete Empty Tracks** option by right-clicking or control-clicking an empty track in the Advanced View timeline.

Customize how clips display in the Advanced View timeline

You can customize the way clips in the Advanced View timeline are shown according to your preferences or the requirements of the task at hand. At the beginning of the clip, you can choose to display a little image called a thumbnail. In addition to showing a thumbnail at the start and finish of the tape, you may also choose to show it constantly throughout (default view). The audio waveform of an audio track's contents can be shown or hidden, depending on your preference.

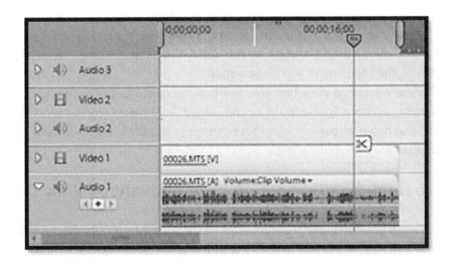

Viewing the thumbnail photographs as they play during the video will give you a good notion of what the tape is about. However, you shouldn't mistake the border between the thumbnails for the actual frame boundary. The thumbnails serve as a rough outline of the video you're viewing, much like a storyboard.

1. Down the left side of the track, you can notice two buttons that say **"Set Video Track Display Style"** and **"Set Audio Track Display Style."** Click a button from this list. With each click, the track's presentation mode will toggle between the different perspectives.

To see additional volume information while viewing an audio waveform in the Advanced View of the timeline, raise the track height.

Saving, Backing Up, and Managing Projects

When you save a project, it remembers your most recent panel configuration, edit decisions, and references to source files. Keep your work safe by saving often.

- Select **File > Save** to save the active project.
- To save a copy of your project, go to **File > Save As,** then enter the name and location of the file, and finally, click **Save**.
- Select **File > Save A Copy** to save a copy of your project so you can keep working on the original. Pick a location, give it a name, and then hit the "**Save**" button.

Tip: Create a scratch disk and assign it the location where Premiere Elements should save all of your project data, including audio and video recordings, previews, and more.

Back up a project with Auto Save

Turning on Auto Save allows you to go back and undo previous edits or recover from crashes. Selecting this option will cause Adobe Premiere Elements to save a copy of your project to the Auto Save folder at regular intervals. You can configure Premiere Elements to automatically save a copy every 15 minutes, for instance. As an alternative to using the Undo function, automatic saving takes into account any modifications made to the project between saves. Archiving several versions of a project takes up less space on disk than storing the original video files since project files are smaller.

1. Choose **Adobe Premiere Elements > Settings** (macOS) and **Preferences** (Windows) **> Auto Save**.
2. Select an option from the following and hit the **OK** button:
   - Select Automatically Save Projects, and enter the duration in minutes, after which Adobe Premiere Elements saves the project.

   - Type a number for the Maximum Project Versions to specify how many versions of each project file you want to save. For example, if you type 5, Premiere Elements saves five versions of each project you open.

Note: Remember to save your work before turning on Auto Save every time you open a new project.

Open an Auto Save project

1. **Do one of these options:**

Get Adobe Premiere Elements up and running. After you reach the Welcome page, choose **Video Editor > Existing Project.** In Adobe Premiere Elements go to **File > Open Project.**

2. Access the file saved by Adobe Premiere Elements automatically within the project folder. (The Auto Save preference might be disabled if there are no files to save.)

Note: Premiere Elements will ask you if you want to open your most recent saved project when you restart the program after a crash.

Project Recovery

Following these steps will bring your Premiere Elements project back to the most recent version you saved:

1. Premiere Elements must be opened after a crash. "**Adobe Premiere Elements quit unexpectedly while a project was open**." is what you'll see in the pop-up.

Caution: The restoration pop-up will not reappear if you dismiss it or the next time the application launches.

2. To restore all the projects to their original condition before the program suddenly ended, choose **Reopen**. The restored project will be saved to the main file with the current changes.
3. Select **File > Revert** to return to the last state that the user saved their project to if they want to see an earlier version of their work.

Tip: Reduce the intervals between autosaves to ensure Premiere Elements frequently backs up your project and reduces project loss in case of a crash.

Recover projects manually

In addition, you have the option to manually restore your projects by following these steps:

1. Find the folder containing your project.
2. A subdirectory called **Recovery Projects** should include a file for every project inside the **Auto-Save folder.** This is the save made when Premiere Pro crashes or is forced to exit.

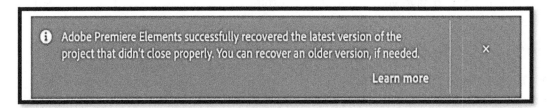

3. If you need to restore to a prior version of an autosaved file, open the **Auto-Save folder** and pick from the many time-stamped versions.

CHAPTER 3
EXPLORE THE PROJECT ASSETS PANEL

Exploring the Project Panel

Once you've dropped media files into the project window, you can organize them any way you like. Media organization in Premiere Elements won't seem so foreign if you're familiar with using folders to arrange files on a computer. The good news is that the process is very familiar to anyone who has ever worked with folders to manage files. Both approaches are similar. Whereas folders are more commonly associated with file organization, bins are more commonly utilized for media storage. You can easily and quickly organize your media files by making bins and then transferring the files into them.

Project Panel Views

Both a **list view** and an **icon view** are available in the Project panel.

The Preview Area

To see media previews, press the menu button in the upper right corner twice. Then, choose Preview Area from the list that displays. Some people think that the Preview Area's information presented to the right of the preview is a benefit.

Navigating the Project Panel

In the Project panel, you can use the scroll bar on the right to go through all of your media files. Navigating through your material is as easy as dragging and dropping. You can go down the page to see more content by using the scroll bar.

Choosing Between Clips

There are many ways to choose clips on the project panel:
- To choose a clip, click on it.
- Press and hold **Shift** while clicking to choose adjacent clips.
- To select clips, press and hold the **Control** key while clicking on them.
- Select several clips in the Project window by dragging them across the screen.
- To choose every single clip in the Project panel, navigate to the **Edit menu** and then choose the **All Clips** option.

Renaming Clips

- Select the clip you want to rename, and then click the right mouse button. Choose to rename it.
- After that, select the text area that lies either below or to the right of the clip thumbnail, according to the situation.
- Once the new name for the clip has been entered, press the **Enter** key.

Copying and Pasting a Clip

- Pick the click you wish to copy.
- Following that, you can choose **Copy** by right-clicking or go to **Edit > Copy**.
- You can either right-click on the bin and pick **Paste** from the context menu, or you can go to the **Edit** menu and select the **Paste** command.

Deleting a Clip

- Select the clip you want to delete.
- After right-clicking on the clip, select **Clear** from the context menu. Additionally, the **Edit** menu offers the option to select **clear**.

Finding Clips

When you need to find a clip in Premiere Elements, you can use either the Find box or the Find dialogue box. Still, using the Find box is the fastest way to go.

Find Box

- You can locate the Find box on the Project panel, so you can use it to search for clips. You may narrow your search to only visible clips in the Project panel, all clips' metadata, or just the speech-to-text metadata by using the In dropdown option, which is to the right of the Find box. The Find box is on the right side of the menu.
- Fill out the search box with a term.

Find Dialogue Box

To access the Search dialogue and look for clips, click the Find button in the Project panel's bottom right corner. Pick a metadata field from the drop-down menu in the Column section. If you'd like, you can add other criteria (a different search phrase) in the row below this one. Once **you are done choosing all of your criteria click the "Match" dropdown menu and choose whether to:**

- Find any content that meets both of those requirements.
- Locate any content that satisfies any of the criteria.

You also have the option to choose whether or not you want the results of your searches to be case-sensitive. After you have completed it, you should click the **Find button.**

Using Bins to Organize Your Media

Bins are what you make use of in Premiere Elements to store and manage your media files. In Windows, bins provide a purpose similar to that of folders.

Creating Bins

Simply making folders is the first step in making bins to store your materials. From the main menu, select **File > New > Bin** to create a bin. Another option would be to access the Project panel and then select the **new bin button**.

Naming Bins

You can start putting the name of the bin into the text field. Make sure you hit the **Enter key** once you finish.

Putting Clips in Bins

Click and drag the clip until it is positioned over the bin you like to add it to. Then, click and hold to add the clip to the bin. Release your grip on the mouse button. Afterwards, in the List view, the clip will be shown beneath the bin.

Viewing Content in a Bin

When you double-click on a bin, you can see what's within. If you want to make a sub-bin, you can do that by selecting the **Create Bin button** in the box up there. Similar to how subfolders work, sub-bins organize and store smaller files.

Setting Bin Preferences

Premiere Elements gives you the freedom to choose several bin-related choices, such as the way bins are opened and other settings. To adjust the bin's settings, go to the menu bar and select **Edit > Preferences > General**. Within the Project panel, you can find the bin by default, but you can change its position in the Preferences menu to open it in a new tab if you want. This is contained within the same image as the Project panel. By specifying the action to be executed when pressing **CTRL+click** or **Alt+click** on the keyboard, you can also configure your keyboard shortcuts. This is an additional option.

About List View in the Project Panel

You can easily find what you're looking for in Premiere Elements' List view, which is under the Project panel, by using the option to categorize the information into categories. When you go to List view, you can pick and choose which columns to display. We can see things like Name, Frame Rate, Media Start, etc. right now.

- Click the arrow in the top right corner of the panel to access the menu of the Project panel.
- Pick Metadata Display.
- To display the columns in that category, just put a checkmark next to them.
- Make sure to select the **OK** button once you are finished.
- You can also remove categories (columns) from the Metadata Display dialogue box by clicking the check box and then choosing "**Remove**" from the context menu.
- After you've decided which columns to display, you can use the dialogue box up top to make your selection. After that, you can arrange and search for content by column by sorting it.

- Selecting a column for sorting is as simple as clicking on its name. To the right of each column name, you'll see a triangle that represents the sorting option—upward or downward. By clicking the name of the column again, you can alter the sort order of the columns.
- To rearrange the columns, simply click on the one you want to move. Next, use the arrow keys to move the column. Move it to the desired spot by dragging it. You will see a blue indication that will point out the location where the column will be put into the spreadsheet.

About the Icon View in the Project Panel

When it comes to organizing content, a list view is useful. On the other hand, the icon view works well for pursuing your stuff. While you are in Icon view, you have the option of seeing the content of source clips in one of two different styles. When you pick a clip while in Icon view, a scroll bar will arise. You may use this bar to travel over the clip and investigate different portions of it. You may even specify in and Out points. The portion of a clip that will be employed in the video project that you are working on is designated by in and Out points, which are used to identify the beginning and conclusion of that piece. The process of editing may be sped up greatly by employing this strategy. You can get the Icon view by heading to the panel menu and selecting the Icon view option. By picking the option labeled "**Sort Icons,**" you can organize the icons in the Icon view. Clicking on a clip to choose it will allow you to see a preview of it in the Icon view. Underneath the clip, you will see a scroll bar that has a playhead linked to it. You can also navigate the footage by dragging the scroll bar up and down while you watch it. If you want to relocate the playhead to a certain spot, you may do so by clicking anywhere in the orange area.

Marking In and Out Points in Icon View

The process of marking in and out points is not as challenging as it first seems. To set an In point in your video, go to the location in the timeline where you want the clip to begin playing. You may locate the spot you're looking for by clicking in the orange area of the tape, or you can play, fast-forward, or rewind the video. Go to the Marker menu and choose "**Mark In**" to make that point the in point. To determine where the Out point is, choose **Marker > Mark Out** from the menu.

CHAPTER 4
THE BASICS OF VIDEO EDITING

Learn the ins and outs of Adobe Premiere Elements video editing with this Quick Guided Edit. You can make rapid work of basic file edits by following this guided edit. **This guided edit will help you accomplish the following tasks more efficiently:**

1. Adding clips to your video
2. Splitting a clip
3. Trimming a clip
4. Publish your finished video
1. **Accessing the Guided Edit:**

To access the Guided Edit, go to the "**Guided**" area and pick "**Getting started with Premiere Elements.**" This guided edit is a step-by-step instruction that tells you how to conduct fundamental video editing operations. You can move forward or backward through the guided edit steps by using the "**Back**" and "**Next**" options.

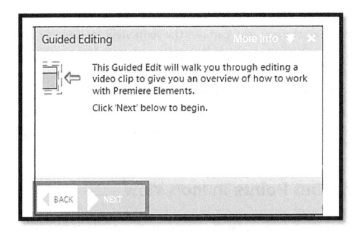

2. **Video Playback Controls**:

Get to know the controls for playing videos. With these tools, you can play or stop your video, which helps you look at it more attentively while you're editing.

3. **Understanding the Timeline**:

The Timeline is shown by the film strip below the video window. By moving the **"CTI" (Current Time Indicator)** left or right, you can move through your video and see previews of different parts of it.

4. **Changing the Length of a Video Clip**:

To get a better focus, change the length of your video clip. You can see more frames of the video by moving the slider to the right. If you slide it to the left, on the other hand, the video gets shorter.

5. **Trimming Video Clips**:

When trimming a video clip, follow these steps to remove any unnecessary footage from the beginning or end:

- Select the exact video clip you want to cut.
- You can remove the clip's end by dragging its right edge to the left. To remove the start, move the left edge over to the right.
- The glimpse in the timeline transitions to reveal the cutout segments from the source video.

6. **Splitting Video Clips**:

To split a video clip into two parts, just positions the CTI where you wish to cut it and then click the **scissors** button. With this action, you can split a single video clip into two independent ones.

7. **Adding Transitions for Smooth Playback**:

You can improve the viewing experience by adding transitions to make the change between video clips smoother:

- The **"Transitions"** choices can be accessed through the action bar.

- Drag and drop the desired transition effect to create a seamless transition between the two videos.
- Use the Transitions Adjustments box to fine-tune the length and location of the transitions for a distinctive look.

Note: If you double-click the transition button on the calendar, you can adjust the settings for the transition at a later time.

8. **Exporting Your Edited Video**:

When you're done making changes, click "**Publish + Share**" to send or share your movie clip. Select "**Computer**" from the list of options, edits the settings and position as desired, and then click "**Save**" to save the altered movie to your computer.

Create a Picture-in-Picture Effect

A picture or video clip can be superimposed onto your movie using a picture-in-picture guided edit. As the video plays in the background, it appears on top of the clip. **To create a picture-in-picture using this Guided edit, follow these steps:**

1. To overlay a video or image on top of an existing one, this Guided Edit will show you how. You can advance through the phases of the guided edit by clicking **back** and **Next**.

Creating a Picture In Picture

Adobe Premiere Elements allows you to place a graphic or video over top of a background video. This feature is called Picture-in-Picture.

In this exercise, you will superimpose a video clip over a background video.

2. Click "Add media" to bring in the video clip you adds scores. If the video clip is already on the agenda, don't worry about it.
3. Choose the option to add media.
4. Go to **Guided > Creating a Picture in Picture.**
5. Move the CTI to where you want the Picture in Picture effect to start.
6. To make one video the background, open it in File Explorer and drag it to the desired location.
7. Select the "**Picture in Picture**" option.
8. The duration can be entered in the **Picture in Picture** text box. In the picture effect, you have the option to adjust the duration of the picture.

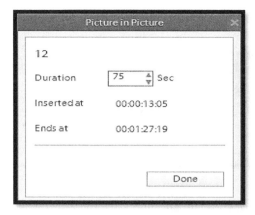

9. Adjust the position of the overlay, and drag the desired location in the Monitor panel.
10. To resize or rotate the overlay, just drag the handle in the corner of the video or image. Click on "**Done**."

Trim & Split Clips

If you want to trim some unnecessary frames from your video, you can use this Guided edit:
1. Use the **Next and Back** buttons to go forward or backward through the guided edit stages.

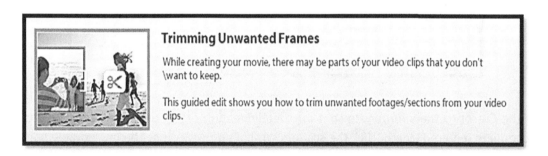

Trimming Unwanted Frames

While creating your movie, there may be parts of your video clips that you don't \want to keep.

This guided edit shows you how to trim unwanted footages/sections from your video clips.

2. Click on "**Add media**" to bring in the video clip you wish to trim. Disregard the video clip if it is already in the timeline.
3. Determine whether to import media.
4. In the Directed menu, choose **Trimming Unwanted Frames.**
5. "**Guided Editing**" appears as a notice. You can adjust the size of the information window. To move to the next stage of the guided edit, click **Next**.
6. Click the left edge of your clip and drag to the right to start trimming from the beginning. The display shows the frame you are cutting to.

7. Click the right edge of your clip and drag it to the left to trim the end.
8. On top of that, you can cut out specific frames from a longer video. To erase the desired piece of the clip, divide the clip into sections and click the scissors sign on the Screen. Place the CTI at the start of the unwanted segment of the video. To divide this video clip into two pieces, click the **scissors** icon on the CTI.

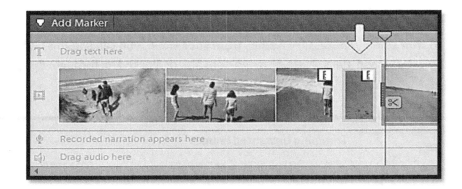

Drag the Cursor to the appropriate spot for the elimination of the undesired region. To trim to the complete required length, click the scissors symbol on the Screen. The unfavorable portion is marked.

Add Transitions between Clips

The cut occurs abruptly when you play the movie and place two different video clips side by side. A smooth transition can be achieved by including a transition between the two clips. **Follow these steps in this Guided edit to create seamless transitions between different parts of your video:**

1. Use the **Next and Back** buttons to go forward or backward through the guided edit stages.

2. Click on "**Add media**" to bring in the video clip you wish to edit. Disregard the video clip if it is already in the timeline.
3. Select the media import option.
4. Under "**Guided**," choose **Adding Transitions Between Video Clips**
5. On the action bar, choose **Transitions**.
6. Look through the available transitions. Drag and drop a transition between clips by clicking on it.

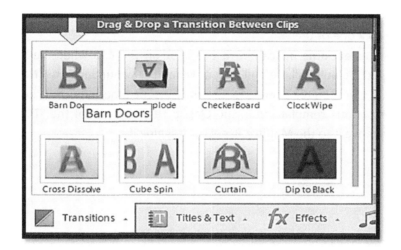

7. To specify how you want the transition to be played, enter the **Transitions Adjustments.** Choose the alignment for the transition and indicate how long it should last.

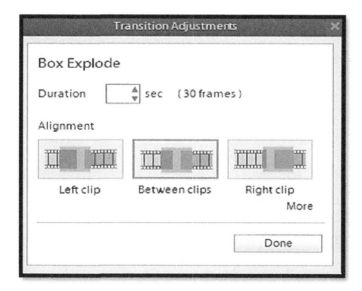

Add a Title to Your Movie

Your video clips have titles, and you can adjust the fonts and colors as well. You may pick from two sorts of titles to put in your movie. Motion titles and Vintage Titles are also available. With Traditional Titles, you may pick and choose specific parts based on your needs. You have the convenience of customizable templates with Motion Titles.

Adding titles

To give it a title, pick one of these:

- Drag the current-time indication to the spot on the clip where you want the title to show. Select Default Still, Default Roll, or Default Crawl under **Text > New Text.**
- Make sure the monitor panel can see the current-time indication by placing it on the clip. Select a title template from the Classic Titles section of the Titles and Text panel, and then move it to the Monitor Panel by dragging it.

CHAPTER 5
APPLYING EFFECTS AND ENHANCEMENTS
Introduction to Effects and Where to Find Them

When it comes to making video projects more interesting and aesthetically pleasing, effects are vital. The effects panel in Adobe Premiere Elements allows you to apply various filters, transitions, and color tweaks to your video files. Your video quality and ability to stand out may be greatly enhanced if you know where to look for and how to use effects. Learn the basics of using effects and where to find them in Premiere Elements with this handy tutorial.

What Are Effects in Premiere Elements?

Preset tools called effects let you edit and improve video footage or give your project a unique twist. From the most fundamental controls like brightness and contrast to more creative ones like blur, antique filters, or styled appearances, the options are almost endless. A wide range of effects are available in Premiere Elements for use in making color corrections, lighting adjustments, transitions between clips, and animations of all kinds.

Types of Effects

1. **Video Effects**: These include filters and adjustments you can apply directly to a video clip. Examples are color correction, noise reduction, and sharpening tools.
2. **Audio Effects**: When you edit audio, you can use effects to make the songs sound better or change them altogether. Some examples include audio balance, pitch adjustment, and reverb.
3. **Transitions**: You can improve the flow of your video by using transitions, which are inserted between clips to generate seamless movements like wipes, zooms, or fades.

Where to Find Effects in Premiere Elements

In Adobe Premiere Elements, you can easily find and utilize effects by following these steps:
1. **Open the Effects Panel**: To access the Effects panel, locate it on the right side of the editing area. To make it visible, locate it in the "**Window**" menu located at the top of the screen and choose "**Effects**" if it isn't already displayed.
2. **Browse through Categories**: For your convenience, the Effects panel is subdivided into many categories. Sections like Transitions, Video Effects, and Audio Effects are all there.

Subcategories inside these main groups house effects such as Stylize, Blur & Sharpen, Adjust for video, and Delay and Reverb for audio.

3. **Search for Specific Effects**: Use the search box at the top of the Effects panel to find a specific effect if you have one in mind. When searching for anything specific, try using terms like "blur" or "**color correction**" as keywords.

4. **Preview Effects**: When you hover over an effect in the panel, a short explanation or preview of its functionality will appear. You may choose the appropriate effect for your video without applying and testing each one individually.

Add Audio and Video Effects

Overview

You can make Adobe Premiere Elements seem better by adding and previewing effects, applying video and audio effects, removing haze manually, adding creative effects, and much more.

Apply and preview effects

As soon as you add an effect to a clip, its parameters are reset to their default values, and the effect stays on for the whole clip. After applying an effect, you may modify its properties in the Applied Effects window. Keyframes allow you to set the start and end times of an effect, as well as change its values over time. You may apply several effects to a single clip, and each effect instance can have its own set of settings when applied numerous times to the same clip. However, bear in mind that the time required to create the final movie will increase in proportion to the number of effects you use. If you find that an effect is inappropriate for your current project, you may easily remove it from the Applied Effects tab.

Apply and preview a video effect

Here are the steps:
1. Press the **Effects** button on the Action bar to open the Effects panel.
2. Pick the filter you want to use on the image. To localize an effect, one must:
   o Select a category of effects from the drop-down menu, and then select the required effect from the list of effects that matches that category.
   o Type the name of the effect you want to find into the search box.
3. Pick up a single clip or many clips to work with in either the Quick view or the Advanced View timeline.
4. You can apply the effect to the clip by dragging it onto it from the Monitor panel, the Advanced View timeline, or the Quick View timeline.

5. Press the **Play button** in the Monitor panel to get a preview of the footage with the effect you just applied.
6. If you want to alter the parameters of the effect, use the Applied Effects tab (this step is optional).

Apply an audio effect

Here are the steps:
1. Press the **Effects** button on the Action bar to open the Effects panel.
2. To add an effect to the recording, choose the sound effect. In the drop-down menu at the top of the screen, locate the Audio Effects category to locate an audio effect. To find the effect, you can also use the search bar. Just type the name of the effect into the box.
3. Select a clip or many clips to work with on the Advanced View timeline.

Note: If you want to choose clips that aren't in any particular order, you'll have to use the control or command key on each clip separately. To select several clips at once, open the Project Assets panel and click and drag a marquee around them.

4. To apply the audio effect to the clip's soundtrack, just drag it to the timeline of the Advanced View.
5. Just double-click the clip in the Project Assets panel, and then press the **Play button** in the Preview window to hear a sample of the audio effect. Keep in mind that to access the controls for playing back the audio, the selected clip must include audio.
6. To adjust the parameters to your liking, just open the effect in the Applied Effects panel and tweak the settings to your liking.

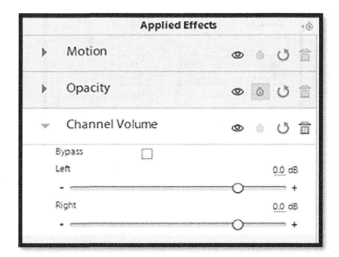

You can turn an audio effect on or off in response to the keyframes you choose by using the bypass option that is included with each effect.

Remove haze, fog, or smog from a video

Particularly helpful for films featuring landscapes, this feature allows you to lessen the effect of environmental or climatic circumstances on your recordings. Haze, fog, or smog may make masking less effective; the Haze Removal filter can help with that. **This Haze Removal filter can be used with one of these applications:**

Manual haze removal

1. You can add a video to the timeline using either the Quick or Expert option.
2. **Do anything from the list of possible things:**
   o After clicking the Effects tab in Quick View, a drop-down menu will appear; from this, choose **Video Effects**. Select the **Haze Removal effect**, and then drag it onto the video you want to edit.
   o To access **Advanced Adjustments**, go to the **Effects** tab in Advanced View and choose it from the drop-down menu. Select the **Haze Removal effect**, and then drag it onto the video you want to edit.

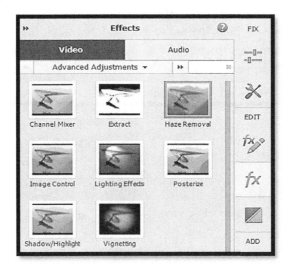

Another way to find the effect is to type **"Haze Removal"** into the page's search bar.

3. The video seems to have much less haze or fog after processing. You have the option to go back to step 2 and apply the effect to more movies if you choose.

Another option is to go to the **Applied Effects** menu and choose **Haze Removal**. From there, you can manually modify the haze reduction level using the Haze Reduction and Sensitivity sliders. You have to turn off the Auto Haze Removal option before you can use the sliders.

- A video's haze or fog level can be adjusted. Commonly referred to as "**haze reduction.**"
- The **sensitivity** parameter dictates the level of haze that should trigger the application of haze removal. The intensity of the haze reduction is proportional to the sensitivity level. When dealing with concerns about sky regions, this is mostly used. If the haze is cleared more aggressively, there can be more noise in the sky.

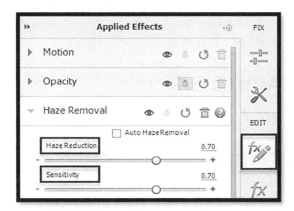

4. Toggle the symbol that resembles a switch to see how well the Haze Reduction feature is affecting the footage.
5. On the Applied Effects panel, either remove the effect or hide it using the toggle button to undo the haze removal.

Auto haze removal

1. Open a movie in Premiere Elements. Put the **Haze Removal** effect on the video when you're in the Expert or Quick modes.
2. Select **Haze Removal** from the Applied Effects tab.
3. To automatically calculate the amount of haze removal depending on the video's haze level, use the **Auto Haze Removal** option.

Be careful not to use the Haze Reduction slider if you've chosen the Auto Haze Removal option. Regardless, you can still tweak the findings by using the Sensitivity slider, which will remain active.

What are Artistic Effects?

You can now alter your recordings with effects inspired by famous works of art or popular art styles with this new video effect called Artistic Effects. Choose from twenty-four unique artistic styles and apply them to your films or still photos.

Steps to apply Artistic Effects

Begin by adding your video clip

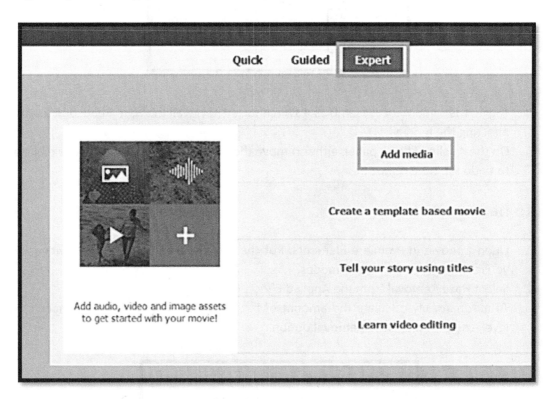

Launch the **Adobe Premiere Elements Editor**, and then choose either the Quick or Expert mode. Just choose the video clip that you want the artistic effect to be applied to by clicking the **"Add Media" button**.

Add Artistic Effect

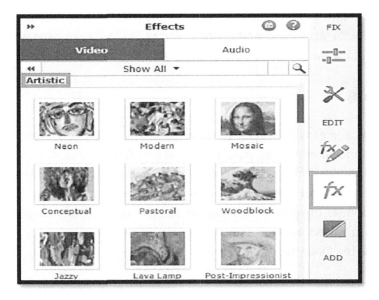

Simply click on the effect's icon on the right side to apply it. Choose an effect from the list in the Video Effects section's Artistic Effects area. Keep in mind that each video clip on the timeline can only have one style applied to it. Still, you may apply the chosen artistic style to any clip in the timeline by dragging and dropping it into the screen. To change a clip's Artistic style, just drop a different Artistic style onto it.

Adjust the effect intensity

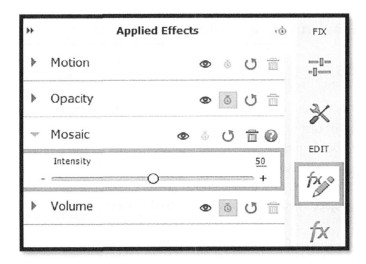

You can find the intensity slider immediately beneath the style you've applied when you click the Applied Effects button on the right panel. To fulfill your requirements, you can modify the amount of creative flare given to your content. Simply pressing the **play button** will reveal the finished assignment. Select **Export and Share** from the **File** menu to export the final file. **Note:** Render the video in the timeline if you would want it to play back without any issues.

Effect presets

Premiere Elements comes with several effect presets. You may apply these presets, which are standard, predetermined effects, to clips. Using the Tint Blue setting, for instance, will give the whole image a faint blue tint. Presets allow users to get good results without having to mess with the settings' properties. Once you've applied the preset, you may tweak it to your liking. You may also customize the parameters to your liking. You can locate all of the effects presets that are currently installed on your computer in the Presets category of the Effects panel. For organizing presets, the following categories are utilized:

Bevel Edges

You have the option to make the picture frame's margins thick or thin.

Blurs

Use your editing program to blur the starting and finishing points of a clip to different degrees.

Color Effects

Make tints that span a spectrum of colors and levels of darkness.

Drop Shadows

Shadows can be either static or dynamic, depending on your preference. Presets for shadows may have a direction of cast or movement indicated by the suffixes appended to their names. As an example, the symbol LL indicates that the shadow is cast to the lower left. Hyphenating the appendix allows it to adapt to changing shadows. Given this, LR LL reveals that the shadow moves from the bottom right to the bottom left. Before applying shadows to photographs that are too big for the project's frame, make sure the background isn't dark. This will ensure that the shadows are seen.

Horizontal/Vertical Image Pans

Create animations where the whole scene moves in a zigzag pattern while the video plays. As an example, the image would be moved from left to right using a horizontal pan from left to right.

Horizontal/Vertical Image Zooms

Create animated zoom effects.

Mosaics, Solarizes, and Twirls

Depending on your preference, create animated effects that gradually increase in strength as the clip goes along or gradually decrease in intensity as it approaches its finish.

PiPs

The target clip has to be shrunk to the right proportions before it can be superimposed over a full-sized clip to achieve a Picture-in-Picture effect. You can also use this effect on many clips simultaneously to create a montage.

Apply an effect preset

When you add a preset to a clip, the following criteria will be used to update it if the preset contains effects that were previously applied to the clip:
- After you apply a preset effect, the parameters of the new effect will take the place of any fixed effects in the preset, such as Motion, Opacity, or Volume.
- If the effect preset contains a standard (non-fixed) effect, the effect will be repositioned to the very end of the effect list.

1. Press the **Effects button** on the Action bar to bring up the Applied Effects window.
2. Whether you're using the Quick View or the Advanced View of the timeline, open the Presets category and drop an effect preset into a clip.
3. To see the effect in action, find the **Play button** on the Monitor panel and press it.

Create an effect preset

Make presets with only one effect or a plethora of them. After applying a custom effect preset, it will be stored in the Effects panel's My Presets area.
1. To save a preset, choose the clip that is already playing with the effect.
2. The Applied Effects panel can be accessed from the toolbar by clicking the **Applied Effects button.**

3. Click "**Save Preset**" after selecting an effect by right-or control-clicking on it.
4. You can name your preset and then click the **Save button** in the dialog box that appears.
5. It is optional but you can describe the preset.
6. Choose how Premiere Elements will handle keyframes when you apply a preset to a target clip by selecting one of the following preset types and then clicking the OK button:

Scale

It scales the source keyframes by the length of the target clip. Any existing keyframes on the selected clip will be deleted by performing this step.

Anchor to In Point

Adjusts the starting keyframe of the preset so it is uniformly spaced between the source clip's In point and the target clip's In point. Selecting this option will create a keyframe one second before the target clips In point, and all subsequent keyframes will be added relative to that location, without scaling. When you save the preset, it takes the first keyframe from the source clip's in point plus one second. This option allows you to add a keyframe from the target clip's in point plus one second.

Anchor to Out Point

Sets the last keyframe to the same distance from the target clip's Out point as the original clip's Out point, ensuring that the position is maintained. To illustrate the point, if the initial keyframe you saved as a preset was one second away from the source clip's Out point, then choosing this option will add a keyframe to the target clip at the same location, along with all the other keyframes relative to it, without scaling.

Adjust Applied Effects

Remove an effect

Here are the steps:

1. Select the clip in the timeline that has the unwanted effect in either the Quick view or the Advanced View. The Advanced View timeline is where this will be executed.
2. Select the effect in the Applied Effects panel. Then, click the Trash bin next to it.

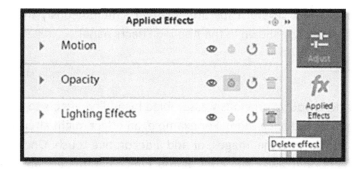

Remove all effects

Here are the steps:

1. To remove an effect from a video clip, choose it in the timeline's Quick view or Advanced View. To choose several clips at once, hold down the **shift** key and click on each one.
2. Select a video clip by using the control key or the right mouse button.
3. Pick the "**Erase Effects**" option.
4. From the options provided, choose an alternate:
   - Video Effects
   - Audio Effects
   - All Effects

Temporarily disable an effect in a clip

If you would want to see the movie without any audio or visual effects, you can disable them.

1. Select a video to see in either the Quick or Advanced View timeline.
2. Pressing the **Applied Effects button** will bring up the Applied Effects window.
3. Press the little eye icon next to it to get a preview of the effect. To toggle all of a clip's effects on or off, click and hold the Alt key on your keyboard while you hover over the eye symbol.

View the effects applied to a clip

All of the clips in both the Quick View and Advanced View timelines immediately have the fixed effects applied, which include Motion, Opacity, Volume, and Balance. Both the Applied Effects panel and the clip instance inside the Advanced View timeline display these fixed effects. When you add a standard effect to a clip, it will show up in the same order that you added it.

1. Use either the Quick View or the Advanced View to choose the video clip on the timeline.
2. The Applied Effects panel can be accessed from the toolbar by clicking the **Applied Effects button.**

Please be aware that when several clips are selected simultaneously in the Advanced View timeline, the effects will not be shown in the Applied Effects panel.

About effects

You can complete a video you've previously assembled by adding effects to certain clips and then rearranging, deleting, or modifying them. For example, an effect might alter the video's exposure or color, tweak the audio, warp the images, or add a decorative touch. Once an effect is applied, you can see its effects right away since all of the effect parameters are set to their default settings. You may adjust these settings to suit your tastes when you apply an effect. With effects, you can do more than just change the clip's size and position within the frame; you can also rotate and animate it. Plus, you're already capable of doing any of these things. You may quickly make edits to your film using Premiere Elements' preset effects. The majority of effects can be customized. However, certain effects cannot be adjusted, such as the Black and White ones. When you apply a theme or make an instant movie project in Adobe Premiere Elements, the application will automatically add effects to your clips.

Standard versus fixed effects

A standard collection of effects can be found in the Effects panel. The Effects panel allows you to apply a wide variety of common effects to any media file in the Quick view or Advanced view timelines. These effects may enhance your video or audio in unique ways or fix common issues like hiss or low light levels. You can add these effects to your audio or images. Both the Quick View and the Advanced View timelines will automatically apply fixed effects to all of the clips. Unless the effect's properties are altered, they will not have any impact on a clip and cannot be removed or rearranged. **Some instances of fixed effects are as follows:**

Motion

You can remove flicker from video footage and also move, scale, anchor, and rotate it.

Opacity

With opacity, you can build fades and dissolves to create your special effects and transitions.

Volume

The loudness of the audio snippets can be adjusted using the volume control.

Balance

Adjusting the volume of individual audio samples is made possible via the Balance function.

Color Correction

AutoTone and Vibrance

Using the in-app controls in Adobe Premiere Elements, the AutoTone effect adjusts the hue, saturation, lightness, and darkness of your video. You have the option to either use the default settings or modify the parameters after applying the effect to a clip. **Note**: Please be aware that the AutoTone settings are automatically applied to every frame; however, the **Vibrance** number must be manually adjusted.

Vibrance prevents colors from being oversaturated once full saturation levels are achieved. As an example, vibrance can be used to prevent oversaturation of skin tones. Colors with less saturation are more affected than colors with higher saturation.

Three-Way Color Corrector

The Three-Way Color Corrector effect allows you to subtly alter the hue, saturation, and sharpness of a clip's shadows, midtones, and highlights. Select the color ranges to be altered using the secondary color correction parameters to further fine-tune your alterations.

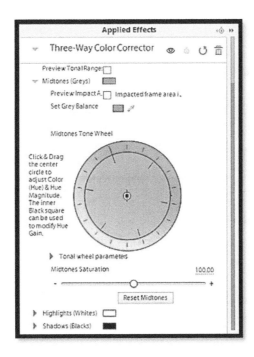

Tonal range

When you use the Tonal Range to preview an image, the **black (shadows), gray (mid tones), and white (highlights)** parts of the image are shown.

Preview impact area

In addition to the locations that have changed, the image changes are shown. As an example, when you adjust the midtones, the altered dark areas of your picture are shown.

Black Balance, Gray Balance, White Balance

Adjust the clip's white balance, mid-tone gray, or black levels. For White Balance, for instance, you would like a hue that is as white as snow. Using the three-way color corrector, you can make the desired color seem white in the picture. To get a sample of a color you want to utilize in the picture, either use the Adobe Color Picker or an Eyedropper tool.

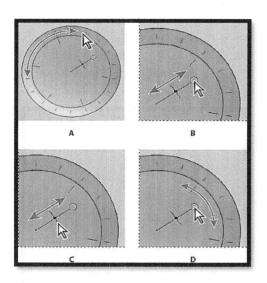

A. Hue Angle **B.** Balance Magnitude **C.** Balance Gain **D.** Balance Angle

Highlights/Midtones/Shadows Hue Angle

Shifts the color to match a certain hue. In its default state, this is set to 0. Values that are positive cause the color wheel to spin to the right, while negative values cause it to spin to the left by one turn.

Highlights/Midtones/Shadows Balance Magnitude

Determines the level of brightness for the video's additional color. Taking the circle further from its center increases its volume or strength. Using the Balance Gain knob, you may adjust the loudness to your liking.

Highlight/Midtones/Shadows Balance Gain

This modifies the range of adjustment for the Balance Angle and Balance Magnitude. Holding the handle of this control near the wheel's center will allow you to make tiny adjustments. To make significant adjustments, shift the handle to the outer ring.

Highlights/Midtones/Shadows Saturation

Highlights, midtones, and shadows may all have their saturation adjusted. With the default value of 100, the colors do not change. Brightness is reduced for values below 100, and all colors are eliminated for values of 0. Color saturation increases as the value rises above 100.

Balance angle

Alters the video's hue to a specified shade. Changing the color is as simple as dragging the Balance Magnitude circle to a desired shade. By modifying the Balance Magnitude and the Balance Gain, one may determine the magnitude of the shift.

HSL Tuner

The HSL adjuster effect allows you to modify the saturation, lightness, and hue of certain colors in a video or picture. **The Applied Effects panel has sliders that you can use to change the hue, brightness, or intensity of the following colors in your image:**
- Red
- Orange
- Yellow
- Green
- Aqua
- Blue
- Purple
- Magenta

You can give your film a cinematic style with the help of the HSL tuner effects.

Split Tone

Make two tones stand out and add blacks to your picture by adjusting the color balance. The Split coloring effect allows you to choose to colorize an image's highlights and shadows. For optimal effects, use contrasting colors for the image's highlights and blacks. The Hue and brightness tools allow you to alter the color and brightness of both the highlights and the shadows.

Temperature and Tint

To make your picture warmer or cooler, you may utilize the Temperature and Tint options in the Adjust panel. You can also change the saturation of the colors green and red in your picture. By adjusting the temperature scale, you can alter the level of blue or orange tone. One way to make a picture seem cozier is to use more color. A cooler tone is achieved by increasing the amount of blue in a picture. You can make the picture seem more green or red by using the Tint tool. **To adjust the tint and temperature of your clip:**

1. **Choose the Clip and Place It**: From the timeline's Quick view or Advanced view, choose the clip whose settings you want to modify. Move the time marker to indicate the start of the selected film on the timeline.
2. **Get to the Adjust Panel**: Click the **Adjust** button from the panel of options on the right side of the monitor. This action opens the Adjust panel, where you may find several tools for making changes.
3. **Change the temperature and tint**: To change the tint and temperature, go to the "**Adjust**" panel and click on the triangle next to the "**Temperature and Tint**" option. The tint and temperature can now be adjusted with much greater precision.
4. **Change the temperature**: Adjust the temperature by selecting the desired shade of blue or orange from the color palette after clicking the "**Temperature**" tab.

To alter the clip's color, just slide the corresponding slider. Changing the temperature to warmer (orange) or cooler (blue) tones alters the video's overall color temperature.

5. **Change the tint**: Select the "**Tint**" tab in the Adjust box to change the tint.

Click on the color choice that corresponds to the tint tone you desire—red or green—to pick it. To adjust the intensity of the tint effect, you can utilize the slider controls. By adjusting the color, the video clip's green or red tones can be changed.

Correcting Exposure and Color Balance

1. **Bring in your footage**: Start a new project with Adobe Premiere Elements.

To begin editing, import the video clips into your project.

2. **Get your workspace in order:** The "**Timeline**" and "**Adjustments**" boxes should be visible from your workstation setup.

To access these panels, go to the "**Window**" menu and click on them.

3. **Change the exposure**: From the timeline, choose the video clip that you want to edit.

Click the "**Adjustments**" tab and then choose the "**Adjust Color**" option. Typically, the "**Exposure**" region is not hard to find. Your options include "**Exposure,**" "**Highlights,**" "**Shadows,**" and "**Contrast.**" Adjust too light or underexposed areas using the sliders. The "**Exposure**" tool allows you to alter the overall illumination.

4. **Fix the color balance**: You'll find these options under the "**Adjust Color**" tab.

Seek for color wheels or scales that deal with "**Tint**" (for magenta or greenish tones) and "**Temperature**" (for warmer or colder tones). Make little adjustments until the colors harmonize. Use the "**Auto**" button as a starting point and then make manual adjustments as needed.

5. **White Balance**: The "**White Balance**" tool is included in Premiere Elements.

You can quickly adjust the white balance by selecting "**Auto Levels**" in the "**Adjustments**" panel. Locate a flat patch of gray or white in your film using the "**Color Picker**" feature if you want greater versatility.

6. **Color Correction Effects**: Premiere Elements offers a wider variety of effects for color correction.

Using the "**Effects**" panel, find the "**Auto Color**" or "**Color Balance**" effect, and then drag it over your clip to automatically modify the colors. Adjust the effect parameters in the "**Effect Controls**" panel for finer-grained control.

7. **Use the Color Correction Workspace**: Navigate to the "**Color**" workspace only for color correction.

This workspace assembles the appropriate panels and tools to facilitate color grading.

8. **Make small changes with Lumetri Color**: As standard with Premiere Elements is a powerful color grading tool named Lumetri Color.

To add "**Lumetri Color**" to your clip, search for it in the "**Effects**" panel. To adjust Lumetri Color's settings (exposure, color temperature, brightness, etc.), open the "**Effect Controls**" panel.

9. **Review and Edit:** Review and edit your changes often to ensure they seem consistent and polished.

Using the "**Program Monitor**" to toggle the display of your modifications on and off will allow you to observe the difference between the before and after.

10. **Save and Export**: Remember to save and export your work as soon as you're through editing.

Choose an appropriate file format and adjust the parameters to meet the requirements of your project.

Advanced Color Correction and Grading

Targeted Color Adjustments

Follow the steps in this Guided Edit to adjust the color, contrast, and brightness of your video footage. **To use this Guided edit to modify certain parameters in your video clips, just follow these steps:**

1. The colors and lighting in your video recordings can be easily adjusted with the help of this Guided Edit.

Adjusting Brightness+Contrast & Color

If the colors in your video seem a bit off or If the lighting does not seem right, you can easily fix them!

Adjust Color, Brightness & Contrast in this Video Guided edit!

2. Click "**Add media**" to add the video clip that you want to improve. If the video clip is already on the schedule, don't worry about it.
3. Pick the option to add media.
4. Select **Guided > Adjusting Color, Brightness, and Contrast.**
5. To edit your video, choose it. Select the video by clicking on it.

Upon selecting the clip, the CTI becomes visible.

6. Select the **Adjust panel** to make changes to your selected settings.
7. Alter the level of brightness and contrast by clicking on **Lighting**.

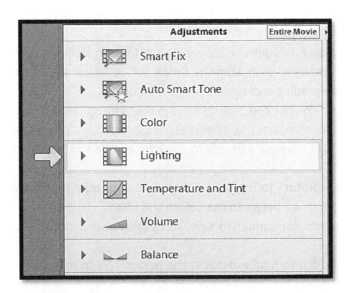

8. To preview the color change, choose an image from the grid in the settings box and click on it. Likewise, to edit an image's exposure or contrast, go to the corresponding tab and click on the image.

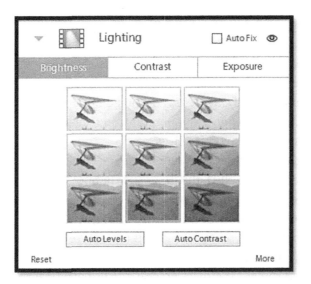

You can make more precise adjustments by clicking "**More**" and dragging the scales.

Note: The clip's brightness and contrast will be instantly adjusted when you choose **Auto Levels** and **Auto Contrast.**

9. To access the Color area, click **Color** in the box of changes. The Color tab allows you to modify the color, brightness, intensity, and vibrance.

You can preview the transformation by selecting an image in the grid.

Advanced White Balance Adjustments

Method 1 - Using the Adjustments Panel

1. **Start up your project**: Launch Premiere Elements and go to the project where the video clip you want to edit is located.
2. **Choose the Clip**: Select the video clip whose white balance you want to modify in your project's timeline. To edit that particular film, you must make this selection.
3. **Get to the Adjustments Panel**: To access the Adjustments panel, go to the dashboard. In most cases, it will be in the area or a different window or tab.
4. **Click on Temperature and Tint**. In the Adjustments panel, you should see the options for Temperature and Tint. Here you can adjust the video's temperature (the degree to which it is warm or cold) and tint (the degree to which it changes colors to green or fuchsia).

5. **Move the Sliders**: Adjust the White Balance using the Temperature and Tint Sliders. Feel free to experiment with the sliders until you get the color balance that best suits your video clip.

Method 2 - Using the Color Panel

1. **Navigate to the Color Panel:** Premiere Elements also has a Color Panel where you can adjust the white balance. Typically, you'll find more color change options in this area.
2. **Click on Temperature and Hue**: A look at the Color panel will reveal the controls for Hue and Temperature. The video's temperature and overall color temperature (Hue) are likewise adjustable in these preferences.
3. **Change the Sliders**: Use the Color panel's sliders—which are comparable to those in the Adjustments panel—to adjust the Hue and Temperature settings to perfection. Play around with the settings until you find the white balance that complements the lighting and overall style of the film.

By using the buttons that allow you to alter the temperature and tint or the temperature and hue, you can effectively alter the white balance of your films. By playing with these sliders and watching the effects, you can get the most precise and visually beautiful white balance for your films.

Achieving Popular Color Grading Trends

Famous color grading techniques in Adobe Premiere Elements are generally achieved with the use of tools like the 3-way color corrector, which enhance and style the photos. **Presented below are the individual steps:**

1. **Initial Color Correction Pass**:

Start by applying the 3-way color corrector effect to your video clip in Premiere Elements. Use this first pass to do fundamental color correction tasks such as modifying exposure, contrast, white balance, and overall color balance. This will help you produce a consistent appearance and solve any issues with the film. To prepare the video for further grading, this step helps get it to a neutral or balanced condition.

2. **Second Pass for Grading:**

Following the first color correction, use the same 3-way color corrector effect for a second pass; however, this time, give more attention to artistic grading rather than corrected modifications.

During this pass, you may achieve the desired effect or adhere to a current color grading trend by using the filter's additional parameters to apply certain color grading styles. Alterations may include adjusting the balance of darks, mid-tones, and highlights to produce a one-of-a-kind appearance; enhancing certain color tones; or using stylized color effects to evoke a specific feeling. For more intricate and professional-level color grading, you may utilize more advanced and specialist software like DaVinci Resolve or applications like Color Finesse. The greater variety of choices and functionality offered by these tools makes them ideal for a wide range of color grading styles and applications. Altering and grading colors in Premiere Elements is a breeze using the 3-way color corrector? Color grading software like Resolve and tools like Color Finesse is great for simple grading tasks, while more advanced grading tasks may need more sophisticated tools. Experts often use these multi-function instruments for precise and nuanced color correction.

Animate graphics

You can learn how to add animated graphics to your movies with the help of this Guided Edit. **To add movement to a graphic element in your video, follow these steps:**

1. Animating graphics has never been easier than with the Guided Edit. Clicking **back** and **Next** will take you through each stage of the guided edit.

Animate graphics easily

In Adobe Premiere Elements, you can easily animate a graphic element across your video.

2. Next, choose "**Add media**" to insert the video file. If the video clip is already on the schedule, don't worry about it.
3. Pick the option to add media.
4. Pick **Guided > Animate** graphics easily.

Note: Only in Expert mode is this guided edit available.

5. Launch the **Graphics panel** from the action bar.
6. To insert the picture, drag the CTI to the desired place in the movie.
7. Place an image on the clip sample by dragging and dropping it.
8. Select the image and then go to the **Applied Effects** section.
9. From the "**Applied Effects**" box, locate the button labeled "**Show/Hide Keyframe Controls**" in the top right corner. Press this button.
10. Click **Toggle Animation.**
11. Modifying the position parameter allows you to alter the animation's position.
12. In the mini-timeline, move the CTI to a spot where you want the image to change or end.

Note: Ensure to make matching keyframes and modify them so you can do this several times.

13. After creating the keyframes that move the image's location, you can enhance the animation even more. Make the picture seem better by adjusting its size and rotation.

Fix Action Cam Footage

Use this guided edit to fix lens distortion, expertly trim, and restore colors in your action cam films.

Fix action cam footage

Follow this guided edit to edit footage shot with an action camera, such as a **GoPro or Phantom**. You can swiftly trim the duration of the camera video using **Smart Trim**. With Color Correction, those vivid hues pop, and the Lens Distortion tool eliminates that pesky fish-eye effect. **Follow these steps to correct the action Cam video using this guided edit:**

1. Click on **Guided**. Navigate to **Video Adjustments**, and then click on **Luma Fade Transition Effect**.
2. Click "**Add media**" to import the desired video file.

If the video clip is already on the schedule, don't worry about it.

3. Pick the option to add media.
4. Select **Smart Trim** from the Tools menu.

Using one of these three video presets, Smart Trim automatically analyzes the footage and selects the best scenes.

People

Observe facial expressions. Perfect for capturing precious family moments on video.

Action

Activity is the main focus. Dance and sports films benefit from it. This default setting is selected.

Mix

Concentrates on a blend of facial expressions, movement, and camera angles. Ideal for films centered on the outdoors and exploration. Changing to a new preset will allow you to have the finest scenes selected automatically.

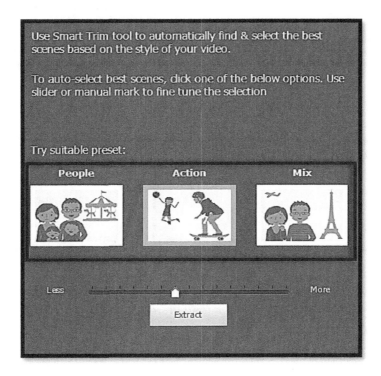

5. To pick several scenes, drag the slider. By dragging the slider to the left, you can choose fewer scenes, and to the right, you can select more.

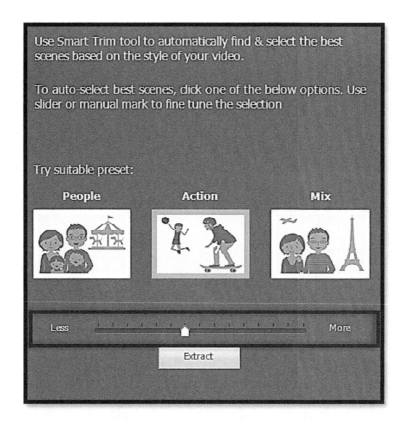

Use Smart Trim tool to automatically find & select the best scenes based on the style of your video.

To auto-select best scenes, click one of the below options. Use slider or manual mark to fine tune the selection

Try suitable preset:

People   **Action**   **Mix**

Less   More

Extract

6. To manually choose scenes, click **Mark Manually** if necessary.

Reset   Mark Manually   ☑ Apply Transitions

Note: Please be aware that by selecting "**Reset**," you will be sent to the beginning of the clip.

7. Press "**Preview**" to display the intended result. Return to make more changes if necessary.
8. To include the selected scenes in the timeline, choose **Export Merged**.
9. Place the Lens Distortion effect on the clip from the Effects panel to fix the clip's lens distortion.

10. To eliminate the fish-eye look, drag the **Curvature slider** to the left.

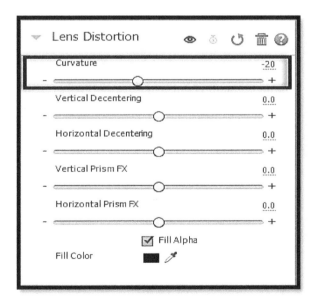

11. Pick **Color** in the Adjustments panel. Finally, from the available presets, choose the appropriate **Hue, Lightness, and Saturation**.

12. Press "**Play**" to see the results.

Note: Shake Reduction might help your video seem steadier.

Fill Frame

Black bars may sometimes appear on the sides of your videos or images. Here, the media's aspect ratio differs from the PRE project's aspect ratio. The items you create may end up looking terrible because of this. If you want the borders of your movies and photographs to match the frame of your video, you may use the **Fill Frame** feature.

1. Once you find the video clip you want to use, click "**Add Media**." It's okay if the clip is already in the timeline.
2. To add media, choose the appropriate import option.

3. Once loaded, the media file is placed in the **Project Assets** bin.
4. To add media to Video 1, open the Project Assets folder and drag the file into the timeline.
5. To the Video 2 track in the timeline, drag and drop the same media file.
6. After you've selected the file in Video 1, go to the right pane and enter the Applied Effects panel.
7. By using the size slider, you can change the size and fill the bars to your liking. Turn up the number until every single bar is filled.

Note: 3X is the optimal scaling for vertical/portrait files and 1.5X for horizontal/landscape files.

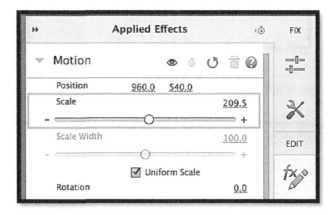

8. To make the sidebar images blurrier, you can use the Gaussian Blur effect. In the right-hand pane, you should see the Effects panel.

A. Applied effects panel **B.** Effects panel

9. Select Gaussian Blur and drag it onto the Video 1 track of your media.

10. Modify the appearance by using the Blurriness slider.

Note: It is recommended to use a blurriness setting of 30. For the majority of media, this works well.

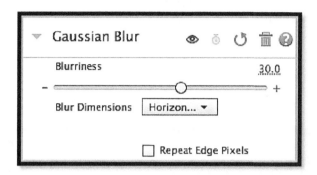

11. To share the final result with another person, go to **File > Export and Share.**

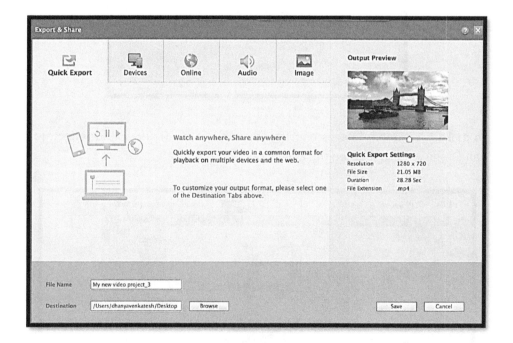

Using LUTs

"**Look-Up Tables**," or LUTs, are fantastic color correction and grading tools in Adobe Premiere Elements. By following these tables—a series of methods for transferring one color space to another—you may get a specific appearance or mood in your video clip.

Here is the lowdown on how to make the most of LUTs in Adobe Premiere Elements:

1. Get to know LUTs:

Types of LUTs: 1D and 3D LUTs are two examples of the many varieties of LUTs. Whereas 1D LUTs alone alter the brightness, 3D LUTs alter both the color and the brightness simultaneously.

Color Correction vs. Color Grading: LUTs have dual functionality, allowing for both color grading and correction. Color correction involves mending and repairing color errors, whereas color grading involves artistically changing colors to achieve the desired effect.

2. Bringing in LUTs:

Finding LUTs: There are a plethora of LUTs, both free and paid, available online. Adobe Premiere Elements requires files with the .cube extension, so make sure to save them in that format.

Adding LUTs is a breeze. With them in hand, go to the Effects panel and go to "**Video Effects**" > "**Color Correction**" > "**Lumetri Color**." From there, drag the "**Creative**" or "**Basic Correction**" effect on your clip to apply it.

Locate your LUTs by going to the Lumetri Color panel, then finding the "**Look**" dropdown option under "**Creative Correction**" or "**Basic Correction**." Click on it, and then click "**Browse...**" to locate your LUTs.

3. Changing the LUT Intensity:

Intensity Slider: A lot of LUTs come with an intensity slider already installed. After using this tool, you may adjust the LUT's intensity to your liking. This allows you to adjust the intensity of the effect.

4. Making changes to LUTs:

Editing LUTs using the Lumetri Color Panel: The Lumetri Color panel allows you to make even more adjustments. Get the style you choose for your film by adjusting elements like color, contrast, brightness, and more.

Adding LUT layers: Try stacking several LUTs or combining them with other color-correcting tools to get your desired effect.

5. Keeping your LUTs:

Exporting LUTs: You can create a unique appearance once and then store it as a custom LUT to use for subsequent projects. Click the three dots next to "**Look**" in the Lumetri Color panel, then choose "**Export Cube...**"

Sharing LUTs: You have the option to share your own LUTs or download LUTs created by other users. Color grading becomes more of a collaborative effort as a result of this.

6. Real-Time Preview:

Performance: Swapping out LUTs may be somewhat resource-intensive. Make sure to choose the "**Full**" quality option before you hit "Send" if you like a seamless playing experience. For instantaneous adjustments, try the "**Half" or "Quarter**" quality options.

CHAPTER 6
AUDIO EDITING ESSENTIALS

About audio mixing

Changing the volume of individual clips and adjusting them to match the loudness of other clips in the project is how Premiere Elements mixes audio. This method ensures that the listener has a harmonious and consistent audio experience throughout the whole film. To lessen the volume difference between the quietest and loudest parts of a narration tape, for instance, you may start by adjusting the tape's level. This allows you to significantly boost the overall volume of the narration, making it stand out against other clips' ambient sounds. Premiere Elements uses the decibel (dB) as its unit of measurement for volume changes. The baseline level of 0.0 dB represents the clip's initial volume, so it's not entirely silent. This causes the volume to drop when the level is set to a negative number and rise when the level is set to a positive one. Several options are available to you for adjusting the volume of a clip. One graph that provides precise control over volume is the volume graph, sometimes called the volume rubberband. A yellow line running horizontally across the audio track of every clip represents it. The Audio Mixer is an alternative that lets you adjust the volume of many tracks simultaneously and has an intuitive interface for managing audio levels. Also, you may keep an eye on the overall volume of your project's audio with the help of the Audio Meters window. This aids in making sure the audio mix remains constant throughout all of the movie's portions and also gives graphic representations of the audio levels. **Here are some things to keep in mind when you adjust the volume levels:**

- If you combine very loud audio samples from various tracks, a staccato distortion called clipping may occur. To avoid clipping, turn down the volume.
- Keyframes allow you to change the volume in specific places within a clip, which is useful if you need to adjust the level of one person's speech to be too low and another's to be too high.
- You can change the clip's volume if its initial level is drastically off by modifying the input level. Keep in mind that if you recorded the footage at a very loud volume, adjusting the input level won't fix the distortion. In some cases, it is advised to record the film again.

Adjust the volume and mix audio in the Audio Mixer

All of your project's audio tracks may have their volume and EQ adjusted using the Audio Mixer. You have complete control over the level and EQ of all the audio in your videos, including the music and any narration. At some times in the video, you may want to amplify the narration while lowering the soundtrack's volume to highlight key details or make sure that any soft voices can be heard over the music. You may watch the video tracks and hear the audio tracks at the same time, allowing you to fine-tune the settings. Proper names are given to each track in the Audio Mixer, and there is a clear link between the two in the **Advanced View** timeline. On top of that, when you make changes to the track, keyframes are automatically appended. You may alter the predefined minimum interval for keyframes in the Audio settings as needed.

Note: It is advised that you use the proper method to blend the volume of one track from start to finish before moving on to the next track. The mixing balance is no different.

1. (This is optional) Select **Edit > Preferences > Audio / Adobe Premiere Elements > Preferences > Audio**, and then specify a value for **Minimum Time Interval Thinning** that ranges from **1 to 2000 milliseconds**. This will restrict keyframes to intervals that are longer than the specified value. Make sure that **Play Audio While Scrubbing** is not selected if you do not want to hear any audio while you are cleaning the audio.

2. Select the Audio Mixer from the Tools panel in the timeline shown in the Advanced view. One alternative is to go to the menu and choose **Tools > Audio Mixer**.

Remember that you can hide or reveal tracks in the Audio Mixer by selecting display/conceal Tracks from the panel's menu and then selecting the tracks you want to display or hide.

3. You may start mixing audio by dragging the current-time indicator to the spot where you want to start.

4. Pressing the Play button in the Monitor window and adjusting the audio mixer's controls will cause the track to automatically add keyframes:

    o   The **Balance** control may be turned left or right by dragging it. This will allow you to change the track's balance.

    o   Moving the **Level control** up or down will allow you to raise the loudness of a particular track.

Note: You have the option to adjust the gap between keyframes in the audio preferences.

Click the **silence button** to silence a track while you are mixing. If you want to momentarily silence the music while you mix, this is the choice for you.

Smart Mix

If the background music in a video clip is too loud and distracting to hear the discussion, SmartMix may automatically adjust the volume. By using this feature, you can be certain that discussions will still be audible even while background music is playing. A well-organized arrangement of your audio components in Adobe Premiere components is crucial for optimal outcomes. Whenever audio is put on either the Audio 1 or the Narration track, it is deemed a Foreground track. And what makes a Soundtrack track a Background track is where the background music is placed. With SmartMix enabled, the application may scour all of the Foreground recordings for audio that pertains to discussions. Then, to make the talks stand out more, the background music is selectively turned down by generating keyframes dynamically. This is because SmartMix automatically creates these keyframes to guarantee that the dialogue placed on the foreground tracks may be heard. Always remember that you can apply SmartMix adjustments to any audio clip in the **Advanced View** timeline, not just the one you've selected. You can't save any keyframes you've already set on the Soundtrack when you apply SmartMix to an audio track. This is because, to prioritize speech over music, the computer adjusts these parameters. Adobe Premiere components automatically adjust the volume of background music and conversational sounds by using SmartMix and arranging audio components on designated tracks. Your video material's audio will sound more balanced and clearer as a consequence.

Change foreground and background tracks

1. **Track Types and Management:** Adobe Premiere Elements automatically assigns a Foreground track to each new track you make. By default, this is how it is configured. Contrarily, track types may be customized to suit your project requirements. Also, you may remove a track from SmartMix processing by enabling it, so it won't be taken into consideration when you make changes to the audio.
2. **Altering the Number of Tracks**: Navigate to "**Tools**" and then choose "**Smart Mix.**" In the Smart Mixer panel, identify the track name. Then, select the dropdown option that is situated below it to alter the track type. Here are three choices for you to consider:
   o **Foreground:** To emphasize the track's status as the project's primary audio element, you may move it to the front.
   o **Background**: To designate a track as a secondary or background audio element, use the "Background" option.
   o **Disabled**: If you want to prevent Smart Mix from processing the track, it will be disregarded when you use SmartMix to edit the audio.
3. **Modifying Smart Mix Preferences**: Selecting the "**Edit**" menu, then "**Preferences**" and finally "**Audio**" is where you can make changes to your SmartMix settings. Within these options, you can adjust several Smart Mix factors, such as:
   o **Define the default track type** (foreground, background, or disabled) when establishing a new track. This is necessary to meet the criteria for the track default. By default, it is configured to generate tracks for the background.
   o **Merge Pause Of:** With the Merge Pause Of setting, you can choose how long a merge should wait before continuing SmartMix processing. The default value is in seconds.
   o **Reduce the Background**: As SmartMix processes, you should decide how much of a drop in volume the background songs should have.
   o **Normalize Dialog**: To make sure the loudness stays the same throughout the whole clip, choose the "Normalize Dialog" option. This will equalize discussions.

With these Smart Mix choices, users may fine-tune their audio tracks to suit specific projects by adjusting the types of files, how SmartMix behaves, and the normalizing settings. By using these tools, you may exert exact control over audio aspects inside Adobe Premiere aspects. With these settings, you may choose which songs to process, which to leave out entirely, and how to adjust the volume of individual recordings.

Apply an audio effect

1. Press the **Effects button** on the Action bar to open the **Effects** panel.
2. Pick the sound effect you want to add to the audio. A drop-down menu will appear; to find an audio effect, choose the **Audio Effects** category. Another alternative is to use the search box to enter the name of the effect.
3. Use the Advanced view's timeline to choose a clip or many clips.

Note: Hold down the **Ctrl or Command key** on each clip to select them even if they aren't consecutive. You may choose several clips at once in the Project Assets tab by clicking and dragging a marquee around the selected clips.

4. Just drop the audio effect into the track that plays in the background of the video in the Advanced View timeline.
5. Press the **Play button** in the Preview window after double-clicking the clip in the Project Assets panel to hear the audio effect before you commit to using it.

The audio playback controls will only appear if the selected clip has audio, so please keep that in mind.

6. Expand the effect in the **Applied Effects** panel to see the settings. Adjust the settings as needed to suit your preferences.

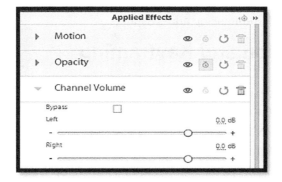

Keep in mind that you can toggle the effect on and off depending on the keyframes you've chosen using the bypass option that comes with every audio effect.

Cleaning Up Audio

If you want to make your audio files sound better in Adobe Premiere Elements, one thing you can do is apply the "**Reduce Noise**" effect. **When you want to enhance the quality of your audio, just adhere to these steps:**

1. First things first, open Premiere Elements and import your media file. Simply put it into the timeline using the mouse to begin working with it.
2. First, go to the effects panel on the right side of the screen. From there, you can apply the **Reduce Noise Effect**. Scroll down to the "**Advanced Adjustments**" area of the menu and find the "**Reduce Noise**" effect.

Select the "**Reduce Noise**" effect from the timeline, and then drop it onto the media file whose noise level you want to lower. As a consequence of applying this effect, your audio will sound cleaner, with less background noise.

3. **Advanced Audio Editing with Adobe Audition**: Adobe Audition, included with Premiere Elements, offers enhanced audio editing capabilities, enabling the use of more intricate settings.

When you right-click on an audio track in Premiere Elements, a menu will open; from there, you may choose "**Edit Clip in Adobe Audition**" to import the clip into Adobe Audition for further editing.

4. **Noise Reduction with Adobe Audition**: To reduce background noise in an audio clip, open Adobe Audition and then find and remove any unwanted noise using the "**Noise Print**" option.

If you want a sample of the annoying noise, you can utilize the **Noise Print** feature. If the noise patterns are consistent throughout the footage, Audition will be able to detect and remove them. Following these steps in Adobe Premiere Elements can help you effortlessly remove background noise and enhance the audio quality of your media. To accomplish more complex and comprehensive noise reduction, it is recommended to utilize Adobe Audition, which offers sophisticated capabilities for enhancing audio aspects.

Audio Automation and Keyframing

Adobe Premiere Elements includes two crucial tools—audio automation and keyframing—in its toolbox. Users may fine-tune the management and editing of audio components in their video productions with the help of these tools. To get expert-level audio results in your video productions, you must use these aspects.

Audio Automation

A feature in Premiere Elements known as "**audio automation**" allows users to dynamically change the loudness of audio clips as they are being recorded. Achieving a precise audio mix throughout the movie, creating smooth transitions, or highlighting important moments are all made easier with this.

The following is how to use audio automation in Premiere Elements:

1. **First, gain access to the audio track**: Before proceeding, make sure you are in the "**Audio**" workspace by selecting it from the workspace bar. This will get you access to the audio track. A view tailored for handling audio components will be shown to you.

2. **Viewing the Audio Track**: Zooming in on your timeline will give you a better view of the audio track, allowing you to examine it in more detail. This makes it far easier to target specific occurrences for loudness adjustments.

3. **Include Keyframes**: Once you've done that, you can start automating your audio. The volume of the audio at certain periods in time is defined via keyframes, which are control points. Adding a keyframe is as easy as right-clicking the audio track and choosing "**Show Clip Keyframes**" > "**Volume.**"

4. **Adjusting Keyframes:** After you've made keyframes, you may alter their positions at any time to determine when the volume changes. You may change the loudness between the keyframes by dragging them up or down. This results in a smooth transition between the different audio levels.

5. **Fine-tuning**: A variety of choices are available to you in Premiere Elements for fine-tuning your automation. The "**Pen**" tool allows you to create custom volume curves, and automation modes like "**Linear**" and "**Bezier**" allow you to change the volume in a variety of ways.

Keyframing

Keyframing is an essential tool for animating various parts of audio and video files in Premiere Elements, and it extends beyond only audio. Aside from audio, it is a technology with other applications as well. Audio professionals rely on keyframes to create dynamic changes in parameters like volume, panning, and audio effects. **Keyframing is a powerful tool in Premiere Elements, and here's how to utilize it:**

1. **Choosing the Property**: Right-click the audio clip and choose "**Show Clip Keyframes**." From this menu, you can pick the property (such as volume or panning) you want to keyframe.

2. **Adding Keyframes**: Similar to the audio automation, you can add important points to the property's timeline by right-clicking on it and selecting "**Add/Remove Keyframe.**" The control points that are created as a result of this action reflect the property's status at that specific moment.

3. **Animating the Property**: You can animate the property by changing the values at different keyframes after you've established them. Manually entering numbers, moving keyframes on the timeline, or, for a more accurate method, using the Effect Controls panel may all be used to do this.

4. **Easing and Bezier Curves**: With Premiere Elements, you can apply keyframe easing for easier and more smooth transitions between changes. You may utilize Bezier curves to further regulate the pace and amount of the attribute changes.

Lastly, Premiere components' audio automation and keyframing provide users full command over their audio components, ensuring a clean and expert sound design in their videos. Editors may enhance their visual narratives with compelling and immersive audio experiences by using these features.

Automating Volume and Effects

In the Advanced view's timeline, you can adjust a clip's volume right on an audio track. For example, by adjusting the loudness graph, you may make a clip's volume match that of its surrounding clips. By using the same procedure, you can completely muffle the footage. **Be aware that keyframes also allow you to adjust the volume.**

1. **Resizing an Audio Track**: To resize an audio track, place your cursor between two tracks in the region of the track header on your computer where you can see the icon for height adjustment. To adjust the audio track's size and visibility, just drag it up or down with the mouse.
2. **Adjusting the Volume of the Clip:** To change the clip's volume, click on it, and then look for the "**Volume**" option in the upper left corner.

To adjust the volume of the selected clip, go to the menu and choose "**Volume**" followed by "**Clip Volume.**"

3. **Accessing the Volume Graph:** You can view the volume graph by hovering your cursor over the yellow line that runs horizontally across the audio track of the clip. The cursor will transform into a white symbol like a double arrow when it is at the correct place.
4. **Apply Changes to the Volume Levels:**

You can make a global change to the clip's audio level by dragging the level graph in either direction. You can also move or drag existing keyframes along the graph to reposition them. As you make adjustments to the volume control, the decibel level will be shown. A negative number indicates a decrease in volume, while a positive number indicates an increase.

Animated Mattes

Animated Matte is a Guided Edit that, when applied to your video, alters its form and look. Select an overlay and apply it to your movie or scene to make it more dramatic.

How to apply animated mattes as overlays to reveal videos

Click on **Guided**, then **Video Adjustments**, and click on **Animated Mattes**. To insert a video, click **Add Media**. To begin adding media, choose the appropriate import option. Once loaded, the media file is placed in the **Project Assets** bin. The media file can be dropped into the Timeline and will be shown on the Video 1 track.

To add animated overlays to this media file, go to the right panel and click on the **Graphics** button. All of the available animated matte overlays will be shown here. You can move the animated matte overlay to a different video track (such as Video 2) on the timeline by selecting it and dragging it there. Place it above the video clip on the Video 1 track.

Note: Adding several overlay clips will provide varied results.

A scissors icon appears on the playhead. When you click the button, the portion of the video without an overlay will be divided. You will be able to retain the rest of the video if you do this.

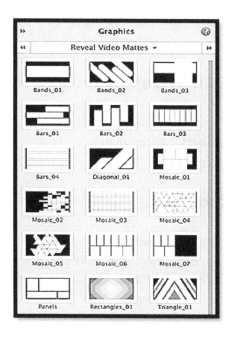

If you want the video to play with the animation, you can use the **Track Matte Key** effect. To add the Track Matte Key effect to a video, find the video on the Timeline's Video 1 track and drag it onto it. After that, go to the screen's right side and click the **Effects** button. **Set Matte** to the video track you added it to (for example, Video 2) and **Composite Using to Matte Luma** in the Applied Effects window on the right side.

You can see the video's stunning presentation by playing it. The last step in sharing your work is to go to **File > Export and Share.**

Use mattes as a transition from one video to another

Transitioning between clips is made possible by animated mattes. Transitions make it simple to go from one clip to another. In addition to splitting parts of a tale, transitions may provide a mood or tone and indicate the passage of time.

How to apply animated mattes as transitions

Animated mattes need a minimum of two video clips to be used as a transition. Hit "**Add Media.**" Pick the appropriate import option, and then drag and drop the files you want to use into the program. Once loaded, the media file is placed in the **Project Assets** bin.

Put the second clip; Clip 2 (the one going out) on   Track 2. Navigate to the **Effects** panel and choose the **Track Matte Key** effect to apply it to a selected clip. By adjusting **Composite Using** to **Matte Luma and Matte to Video 3**, you can modify the parameters of this effect. Next, you'll want to apply the **Reveal Video Matte** to track **Video 3**. Verify that the **Reverse** box is ticked.

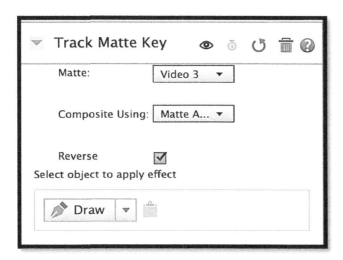

Put the **Reveal Track matte** clip on video track 3. Select **Reveal Video Mattes** from the **Show All** drop-down in the **Graphics** panel. After you've decided on a transition finish, drag it into Video 3 in the timeline and position it so that its end coincides with Clip 2's. With **Timestretch**, you can adjust the speed of the shift.

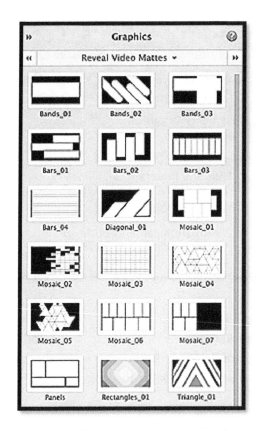

Clip 1 should be placed on track 1 so that its start time lines up with the start time of the **Reveal Track Matte** clip on track 3. To make this clip fade in, right-click on the clip > **Fade** > **Fade In Video**.

Adjust the input level of clips

If the clip's starting volume is too loud or low, you should increase the input level (also called gain) first, before adjusting the output levels. However, increasing the gain will magnify the noise if the original audio's level was too low when recording. The optimal setting for capturing high-quality audio without distortion is a somewhat loud volume. When left uncorrected, the Audio Meters panel indicates that well-recorded audio reaches its peak between zero and six decibels. Clipping occurs when the recording level is greater than zero decibels. In the Advanced view **timeline, you'll find the controls that allow you to adjust the audio gain of individual clips or many clips at once in Adobe Premiere Elements:**

    1. **Choosing Clips:**

Simply click on a clip in the timeline to see its properties and use the **Single Clip Selection** function.

Picking just a few Snapshots

- o Selecting many clips at once requires holding down the **Ctrl** (or **Command**) key (Mac users) and clicking on each clip individually.
- o To make consecutive clips, go to the **Project Assets** panel, then click and drag a selection box around the clips you want to utilize.
- o To select all of the clips in the timeline at the current time, use **Ctrl-A (or Command-A** on a Mac).
2. **Access Audio Gain Options:**

Once you've completed choosing the clips, go to the menu and choose "**Clip**" subsequently to "**Audio Options**" and finally "**Audio Gain.**"

3. **Adjusting Gain**: Two controls allow you to change the loudness of the sound:

Select the zero value and type in the desired gain value to perform a manual adjustment. The clip's original gain, denoted as 0 dB, remains unchanged. Just click the "**Normalize**" button and the gain will be adjusted automatically. To avoid clipping, Premiere Elements can determine exactly what adjustments are needed to raise or lower the gain, so the audio levels are always perfect. Users can adjust the volume of one or several clips inside Adobe Premiere Elements' timeline by following these steps. Users may achieve the necessary audio levels without distortion with the help of choices for precise manual adjustments or automated normalization.

Mute a clip

These are the procedures to take in Adobe Premiere Elements' Advanced view to enable or deactivate audio tracks in the timeline:

1. **Choosing Audio Track:** If the audio is synced with the video, then:

Press the Alt key (or Option on a Mac) in the timeline to choose the clip's audio track. This action just selects the audio component of the linked clip.

Assuming that the audio is not connected to the video

You need to click on the clip to choose it and its audio track.

2. **Enable or disable the clip:** After choosing the full or partial audio clip, you can enable or deactivate it:

Pick the "**Clip**" option from the menu. Select "**Enable**" to toggle the clip's state. After a clip is deactivated, you won't see it in the clip menu anymore, and its name will fade off the track as time goes on.

Removing Background Noise and Enhancing Clarity

You may have seen grains or speckles as a kind of noise in videos before. Possible causes include using a high ISO or shooting in dim conditions. If you want to use the decrease noise effect, then follow these instructions.

1. Premiere Elements allows you to import media files and then drag & drop them into the timeline.
2. Select effects using the panel on the right. A window for video effects opens. You can also use this effect in the Quick view window.
3. Under **Advanced Adjustments**, select **Reduce Noise** and drag-and-drop it to your media file in the timeline.

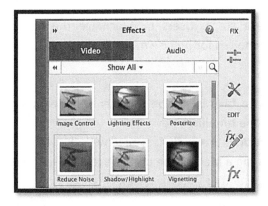

4. From the **Applied Effects > Quality** drop-down, you have the option to modify the output quality.

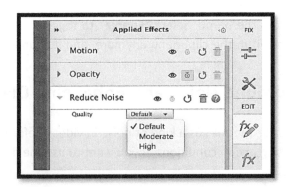

5. To see the outcomes, either export the file or render it.

Adding Background Music

Adding a music score to a video clip

In this context, a "**music score**" is an audio track that may be added to a video in the timeline. A preamble, main body, and conclusion are all part of it. The duration of a video track is dynamically adjusted by the music performed in a soundtrack. Similar to a piece of music, a Soundbooth score can adjust its structure and mix to fit a user-specified intensity level in response to user-specified factors like a video's duration. **If you want to add music score to your video clip, here's how:**

1. Choose **Add Audio to the soundtrack**.
2. Choose "**Music Score**" from the selection that appears. It shows a list of types of musical scores. To listen to samples from a certain kind of musical score, just choose one.

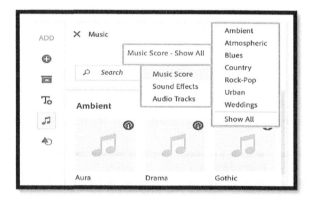

3. The scores are displayed under the music score category selected in the previous step. Click the preview button to hear the score before applying it to the video clip.

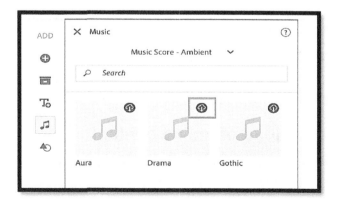

4. Choose the musical score you want to use for the video by clicking on it. Place it on the target video's timeline by dragging and dropping. It brings up the contextual pop-up menu for **Score Property.**
5. Choose one of these choices from the **Score Property** pop-up:

Intensity: Music scores are audio recordings that include the interplay of many instruments. To make these noises louder, move the slider to the "**Intense**" position. To make the music less loud, move the slider to the left until **Mellow** is reached.

Fit Entire Video: To apply the score to the whole video, choose "**Fit Entire Video**" from the main menu. The video clip is accompanied by the score sound.

Choose "**Done**"

6. To listen to the music score after adding it to the video clip, hit the S**pacebar** key or click **Play**.

Repositioning the music score

Because it is a dynamic component, the musical score may be moved and altered in real-time. While moving the score, you have the option to do the following:

Trim the score

Easily reduce the length of the musical score. Use the trim handles to cut the music score at the beginning or end of the chosen area. To make the music score shorter, just slide it inwards.

Stretch the score

By clicking and dragging the end of the score, you can extend its duration. Stretch out the score until you reach the point where you want to incorporate it into the video.

Reposition the score

You can move the musical score around the video by clicking and dragging it to other spots.

Deterministic download of online content

Downloading internet material is made deterministic in Adobe Premiere Elements 2025 and before versions. This means that you can determine the file size of web material before downloading it in its entirety. You can monitor the download status of individual files if you download them one by one. Consider the practice of downloading musical scores as one example. **Here are the procedures to demonstrate how deterministic download works for music scores:**

1. Choose **Audio > Music Score.**
2. Choose a musical score of your choice.
3. If you see the blue bars, it means you need to download the music scores.

Adding sound effects to a video

If you want to add some flair to your video or highlight a certain scene, you can do so using sound effects. These effects are superimposed on top of the video's background. **A video clip can have a sound effect added to it by following these steps:**

1. Import your video clip to the timeline.
2. (In Premiere Elements 2024 and earlier versions, all the sound effects are downloaded by default.) From the action bar, choose **Music > Sound Effects.**

New: Premiere Elements 2025 now supports on-demand content downloads. There is no option to download material manually or using a deterministic algorithm.

3. Feel free to peruse the sound effects by selecting a category from the list.
4. You can listen to a preview of a sound effect by clicking the Play button.
5. To add a sound effect, click and hold it; then, drag it to the timeline's Music track.
6. Use the space bar or click **Play** to see the video with the sound effect.

CHAPTER 7
ADDING TITLES, TEXT, AND GRAPHICS

Even though we don't often give titles much thought, they are an integral part of any video or film, and every video that has ever been made has had one. Titles provide crucial information about the movie that cannot be conveyed via images, such as the film's name, the setting, and the period in which the tale takes place. This tutorial will teach you what you need to know to use Adobe Premiere Elements for title and text editing, including how to make a title with moving text, use a template, and much more. Adding titles to movies is a simple and fast process, even though titles may be artistic creations in their own right. The reason is that most editing programs come with very user-friendly title templates. Adding titles to their flicks is a breeze. Even though you'll need some video editing skills, we'll show you how to use this tool to add titles to your films.

How to Add and Edit Titles in Premiere Elements

As its name implies, still titles don't move around when they're on screen, but motion titles create visual dynamics by moving around. These two categories may be applied to any title. Because the "**Expert**" mode in Premiere Elements provides more options than the "**Quick**" or "**Guided**" modes, it is recommended to utilize this mode when adding titles to your project. Go to the "**Expert**" mode to add titles to your project.

1. **Adding Titles in Premiere Elements**

Verifying the presence of a video clip on the timeline is the first step in incorporating titles into your film. The next step is to go to the part of the video where you want the titles to show up. You won't be able to proceed to the next stage of adding video titles unless you do this. Next, choose the 'Text' menu from the main menu. Then, from the drop-down menu that displays, select the **'New Text'** option. To add a text file to the timeline, choose the **'Default Text'** option from the **'New Text'** sub-menu.

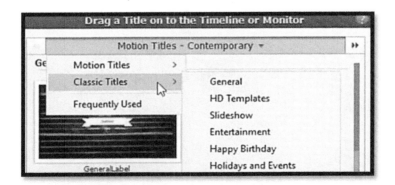

You can add titles to your project in other ways as well. Your options aren't limited to this way alone; Premier Elements' **"Titles and Text"** panel offers a variety of 'Classic' title options as well. After you've chosen the title you want to use, just drag it from the panel into the timeline.

2. **Adding Motion Titles in Premiere Elements and Other Programs**

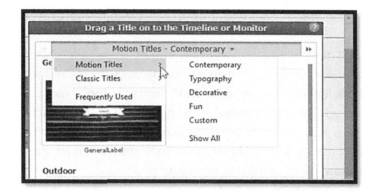

'Motion Titles,' an option in the **'Titles and Text'** tool, allow you to give your document text some movement. Choosing a **"Motion Title"** is as easy as dragging and dropping it into the timeline. Once you've positioned it on the timeline according to your liking, you may customize each motion title to your liking by using the **'Adjustments'** option. If you want to alter the wording, backgrounds, or photographs in the motion title, you can easily do so and save it to use in another project.

How to Create Titles in Premiere Elements

Video editing software like Premiere Elements makes it easy for even the most inexperienced editor to produce professional-looking results, without having to learn every trick in the trade. Ignoring this reality, titling your movies requires some familiarity with video editing software. **The program's interface provides a plethora of title alternatives; let's check them out.**

1. **Motion Title Creation Using Premiere Elements:**

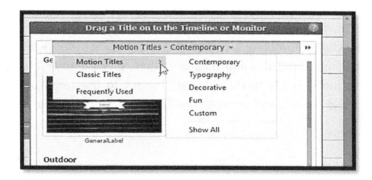

Including moving titles in your films is an easy and entertaining way to make them more engaging. Simply go to the **'Action'** bar, click the 'Titles and Text' button, and from the drop-down menu that displays, choose the **'Motion Titles'** option to create a title similar to this one. Under the submenu, you'll see several options, such as **"Contemporary"** and **"Typography;"** but, you may view all of the **"Motion Titles"** choices by selecting **"See All."** After you've settled on an effect you like, you can simply drag and drop it into the timeline to where you'd want it to appear.

2. Creating Still Titles:

When using Premiere Elements, there are two separate ways to create static titles for your films. Here are some choices for you. Choose "**New Text**" from the "**Tools**" menu; that's one possibility. Within the submenu, you'll find the **'Default Text'** option. After you've clicked the feature to add it to your project, you may enter the text you want to utilize. Alternatively, you can pick the **'Classic Titles'** option from the drop-down menu that appears when you click the **'Titles and Text'** icon on the **'Action'** bar to add still titles to your project.

3. Creating Titles with Animated Text:

Animating text in Premiere Elements is a rather straightforward procedure. First things first: add the title file to the timeline. Only then can you begin animating your project's text. After you've added the title file to the timeline, choose it and then go to the "**Adjust**" tab. A window will pop up; in the next step, click on the "**Animation**" preset that appears in the drop-down menu. To preview an animation before using it, just click on the play button next to its icon. Simply clicking the "**Apply**" button will apply the effect and save your changes.

4. Creating Rolling or Crawling Titles:

Most people, when asked about titles, immediately think of rolling and crawling titles because of how often they appear in movies. You can access the "**New Text**" option in the "**Tools**" menu. The next step is to choose the "**Default Roll**" or "**Default Crawl**" option. The titles for the roll or crawl will be immediately added to the timeline when you complete this step. By moving the title's end, you may adjust its display duration. The longer the title, however, the slower the material within it will load, so keep that in mind. Pressing twice on the title file in the timeline will bring up further customization choices. Make sure the settings are suitable for your needs by adjusting them in the popup that soon follows.

5. Adding Titles to Documents Using the Template

Preset titles often include components that won't work with your project. Following these steps will ensure that your chosen template is customized to your exact specifications for your project. From the **'Action'** bar, find the **'Titles and Text'** icon; then, pick the template you want to use for your project. When you're ready to make some changes to the template, just drag it to the timeline's video track, choose it, and then use the **'Monitor'** panel to make it fit.

Create a title with animated text

Any static title can be easily animated using a preset. Title characters may be easily animated using text animation presets to fly in from the top or bottom of the screen, fade into view, or pop into view. For instance, when you choose the **Fade in by Characters** option, all of the individual characters in your title will gradually come into view until the title is finished. To get a preview of an animation, hover your mouse over the "**Animation**" tab in the Adjust panel.

1. **Pick an action from the list:**
   o Select the clip with an overlay on the Quick view timeline. To modify a clip, just double-click its title text after selecting it in the Monitor panel.
   o Double-click the title clip when viewing the timeline in Expert mode.

You can now see the options for text customization in the updated Adjust panel.

2. To choose an animation preset to apply, open the **Adjust** panel and go to the **Animation tab**.
3. Pick one of these options to apply the preset to the title:
   o Press the "**Apply**" button.
   o Start by dragging the desired preset to the Monitor window and placing it on top of the title text.

Note: You can remove an animation from a title by selecting the title text, and then clicking the **Remove** button (located at the bottom of the Animation tab) in the **Adjust** panel.

Create a title from a template

Some templates include visual elements that might be appropriate for your film's theme, such as a new baby or a vacation. When you're making your movie's credits, you may replace the fake text with your own. Black backgrounds stand in for the transparent backgrounds used in a few of the templates. You may now see your movie playing in the background of the template. There are some that no one can comprehend. Simply choose the text or visual element you want to edit, and then either erase it or write over it, depending on your preference. Adding things to the title is another option you have. The original template is saved with your project once you make changes, but your customized version of the title is not. Just a friendly reminder that any material from previously applied templates will be superseded by the content of any new templates you apply. **Here are the steps:**

1. Select **Titles and Text** from the Action bar's drop-down menu.
2. To access a template, navigate to the program's **Titles and Text** area and choose a category of templates. When making title templates, you can choose between the two timeline views: Quick view and Advanced View.
3. You have the following choices at your fingertips when working in the Quick view timeline:

Simply drag the title template from the **Titles and Text** panel to the desired location in the Quick view timeline to insert it. The existing clip will be moved to the right if it is in the target region so that the new title may be placed there. Pick out a clip to edit in the Quick view timeline. Then, move the template from the **Titles and Text** panel to the **Monitor** panel. The newly selected clip will now have its title applied. To modify a clip in the Quick view timeline, click on it. Then, choose the template you want to use. Lastly, click the **Apply button.**

4. The following choices are available to you while working in the timeline using the Advanced View:

A video track in the Advanced View timeline can have the title template dragged onto it from the **Titles and Text** panel at any point along the track. To create the title, drag the template into the **Monitor** panel after repositioning the indicator displaying the current time to the desired location. To apply the template to a specific clip, go to the Advanced View timeline, find it, and then click the **Apply** button.

5. Make any desired changes to the title.

Apply online title templates

You can get a wide variety of title templates for Adobe Premiere Elements on the internet. **What follows are instructions on how to download and use title templates:**

1. Use the right mouse button or the control key to choose the Title template.
2. Click the **Download Now button** once you've chosen the template you want to download. Alternatively, you can get all of the Title templates by selecting **Download All** from the menu.
3. As an extra step, you can choose to download the content in the background while you work in Adobe Premiere Elements by clicking the **Download in Background** button.

You can download the online content linked to a Title template in Adobe Premiere Elements by dragging and dropping a template from the Title and Text panel onto a clip. The downloaded content is then integrated into the template after that. A blue bar in the item's top right corner indicates that it hasn't been downloaded yet.

Trim titles

If you want to remove every instance of a title from a movie, you can do so using the Project Assets panel. You can easily edit out specific instances of titles by choosing them in either the Quick view or the Advanced View timeline. In the Advanced View timeline, the length of the title instance varies when you trim an instance. Despite this modification, the initial clip's duration under the Project Assets tab will remain unchanged.

Trim all instances of a title

Here are the steps:

1. Select the **Project Assets** panel from the Advanced View by clicking on the associated button.

2. Select it by double-clicking on its title in the Project Assets tab. clicking the title will bring up the Preview box.
3. Take one of these steps in the "**Preview**" pane:

To cut the title, just drag the **Set In or Set Out handle**, as desired. To set a new **In point or Out point**, you need to move the current-time indicator to the desired position, and then click the **Set In button or the Set Out button.**

4. In the Preview window, choose the Close option to finish closing the window.

Adobe Premiere Elements saves the reduced title in the Project Assets tab.

Trim an individual title instance from the Advanced View timeline

Here are the steps:

1. On the timeline for the Advanced View, find the title that has to be shortened and make sure it is in one of the video tracks. You may need to slide the scroll bar on the video track to see the title.
2. Once you've moved the cursor to the start or end of the title, you'll see the ripple trim symbol. After that, you can drag the title's end to make it shorter. On their own, the holes close up. If you have already created a black video clip for your title, you will also need to decrease its size.

Holding down the **Control** key while dragging and clicking the clip end allows you to trim instead of closing the gap.

Create shaped objects for titles

Using the drawing tools provided in the Monitor panel, you can create a variety of shapes, such as rectangles, dots, and ellipses. After you've drawn a shape, you can change its fill and stroke properties and give it a style. **Here are the steps:**

1. To open the title in the Monitor panel, double-click on it in the Advanced View timeline if it isn't already open.
2. The Monitor panel has a menu where you can choose a shape tool.
3. Complete one of these tasks:

To limit the shape's aspect ratio, press and hold the **Shift** key while dragging. Press and hold the **Alt** key while dragging to begin drawing from the shape's center. To restrict the aspect ratio and draw from the middle, press and hold the **Shift and Alt** keys simultaneously while you drag the mouse. The diagonal orientation can be achieved by dragging the shape across the corner points as you design it. By moving the mouse across, up, or down, you can rotate the shape horizontally or vertically as you're drawing.

4. To apply a style to an item, click on it in the Style area of the Adjust panel.

Add images to titles

An image can be used in a title in two ways: as a standalone visual element or as an embedded element inside the text by putting it in a box. Premiere Elements allows users to import both bitmapped photos and vector artwork. Bitmapped versions of vector-based artwork may be seen in the Monitor panel. It is the default behavior for pictures to be shown at their original size when you upload them. You may edit the size and other aspects of an image after you've added it to a title, just like any other object's properties. Titles that feature images are not considered part of the title itself, unlike titles that include text or other visual components. In contrast, the image serves as a reference to the original image file, much as the audio and video files provided in the Project Assets tab do.

Place an image into a title

1. To open the title in the Monitor panel, double-click on it in the Advanced View timeline if it isn't already open.
2. Do an option from the following on the Monitor panel:

Select "**Image**" followed by "**Add Image**" from the menu that displays when you right-click or control-click on the Monitor panel. Choose **Text > Image > Add Image** from the menu. The dimensions of an image are preserved when you import it into Premiere Elements.

3. Simply drag the image to the desired viewing location in the Monitor panel. If necessary, you can adjust the size, opacity, rotation, and scale.

Keep in mind that the dimensions of the screen on which a video project is shown are sometimes much smaller than those of the digital still photos shot with a camera. By moving the image's corner handle while holding down Shift or by using the **Text > Transform > Scale command**, you can resize an image without introducing distortion.

Place an image in a text box

Inserting a picture into a text box causes it to perform just like a text character. When an image is "**floating**" within a text box, this happens. It can take on the appearance of other characters, including strokes.

1. To open the title in the Monitor panel, double-click on it in the Advanced View timeline if it isn't already open.
2. Select the **Horizontal Type Tool** or the **Vertical Type Tool** from the Adjust menu and click on it.
3. To insert the image, click the photo in the Monitor panel's text field to make it the active selection.
4. Do one thing from this list:

To add a picture to the text, choose **Image > Insert Picture into Text** after right-clicking or controlling-clicking the Monitor panel. Choose the **"Text" menu**, then **"Image,"** and then **"Insert Image into Text."**

5. Press the **Open** button once you've selected an image to open.

Restore an image to its original size or aspect ratio

Here are the steps:

1. To open the title in the Monitor panel, double-click on it in the Advanced View timeline if it isn't already open.
2. Once you've made your choice, you can use the picture in one of these ways:
*   Choose "**Text**," "**Image**," **and "Restore Image Size"** from the menu.
*   Pick "**Text**," "**Image**," **and "Restore Image Aspect Ratio"** from the menu selection.

Superimposing titles

After you add a new title, it will appear above the video clip where the time indicator is. Making new titles always works in this way. Conversely, you may choose to place it into a blank area on the Advanced View timeline if there is no existing video. You may transfer the title from its current location to a clip at a later stage. If you make a title in Adobe Premiere Elements and then leave a blank location for it, the computer will insert it onto the Advanced View timeline's Video 1 track and the Quick view timeline's Title track. Keep in mind that the title will vanish from the Monitor panel and the timeline in Quick View and Advanced View will be affected if you drag a clip onto a title or into a track above a title, respectively. If you're using the Advanced View timeline and you set the clip to a track above the title, the same rule applies. Drag the title up the timeline until it's above the track containing the clip; this may be done by clicking the Advanced View timeline button. The visibility of the title will be restored.

CHAPTER 8
TRANSITIONS AND VISUAL FLOW

How transitions work

Using transitions, you may add a stylish beginning or ending to a single clip, or fade out one clip and fade in another. Some transitions are more dramatic, like a page flip or a spinning pinwheel, while others, like a cross dissolve, are more subtle and expressive. It is common practice to add transitions to cuts between segments to generate transitions that are visible on both sides. You can also apply a transition to just the beginning or end of a clip if you want to make a one-sided transition, such as a fade to black.

When the transition happens, the frames from both clips become merged. The overlapping frames may be made up of frames that were previously clipped from the clips, or existing frames repeated on each side of the cut. Clipped frames are those that are barely beyond the in or out point at the cut. Remember that cutting a clip does not need removing any frames. Rather, the generated In and Out points are used to form a window over the original film. The transition effect is created by using the decreased frames in a transition. The transition would repeat frames if the clips did not include clipped frames.

Previewing available transitions

You can access the available transitions by clicking Transitions on the Action bar, which will take you to the Transitions panel.

- **Quick view:** A thumbnail of each potential transition is shown in the Transitions panel. The Quick view includes a subset of the available transitions in the Advanced view.
- **Advanced View:** In the Advanced View, the transitions are organized into categories. From the Category menu, you may narrow your search to transitions by choosing a kind, such as Dissolve. You may also use the name of a transition to find it in the search bar. The number of transitions in the Advanced View is more than in the Quick view.

You can see the effects of a video transition on a clip in an animated thumbnail preview. Select a transition to animate its thumbnail. You can preview an animated thumbnail transition in the Transition panel before applying it to a clip.

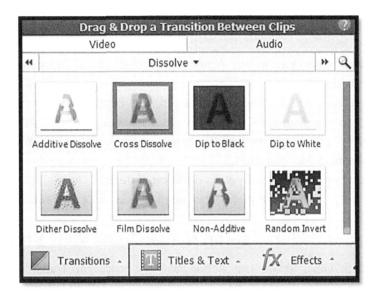

Two audio transitions are offered in Adobe Premiere Elements' Crossfade category: **Constant Power** and **Constant Gain**. Although offering fades, they are distinct in certain ways. Despite being linear in theory, Constant Gain tends to sound abrupt, in contrast to Constant Power's more gradual drop.

1. In either the Quick View or the Advanced View, click **Transitions** on the Action bar. A panel that handles transitions appears.
2. Click on the thumbnail of any video to start the transition.

Specify a default transition

The preset transition is useful for both custom slide presentations and importing PSD files into Adobe Photoshop Elements. Animated DVD menu backgrounds are another possible usage. The usual transitions for video or still images are Cross Dissolve, and for audio, Constant Power. But these options are changeable.

1. In both the Quick View and the Advanced View, click **Transitions** on the Action bar. A panel that handles transitions appears.
2. To make a certain transition the default, right-click or control-click on it and then choose **Set Selected as Default Transition** from the context menu. A gray outline represents the default transition symbol.

Apply transitions in the Quick view timeline

Drop zones, shown by vertical green lines, appear when you move a transition in the Quick view timeline. Quickly switch between clips by using the drop zones.

Apply a double-sided transition in the Quick view timeline

1. In the Quick view, locate the Action bar and click on **Transitions**. The panel for Transitions is shown.
2. You can easily insert a transition between two clips in the Quick view timeline by dragging it to the drop zone in the Transitions panel. A transition sign appears in the bottom right and left corners of the clip to indicate its usage. You can also see the contextual control for Transition.
3. Alter the clip's properties, such as its duration, if desired. To see how your modifications will affect the transition and make more adjustments, click the "**More**" button.

Apply a single-sided transition in the Quick view timeline

1. In the Quick view, locate the Action bar and click on **Transitions**. The panel for Transitions is shown.
2. From the Transitions menu, choose the one you like.
3. Pick out a single option:

To move the transition to a blank area on the clip's edge, just drag it to the transition rectangle. Move the transition to the edge of the clip that you want it to appear on if it's next to another clip. Within the contextual control for Transitions, choose the Alignment option to Left Clip, Between Clips, or Right Clip.

Apply transitions in the Advanced View timeline

When using the Advanced View to add transitions to the timeline, you can choose between three different alignment options: Left Clip, Between Clips, or Right Clip.

Apply a double-sided transition in the Advanced View timeline

To apply a transition between clips in the Advanced View timeline, they must be on the same track and have no gaps between them. To accommodate a double-sided transition that uses repeated frames instead of truncated ones, the transition icon has extra diagonal lines. The lines encapsulate the region that made use of the repeated frames.

1. On the Action bar of the Advanced View, click **Transitions**. A panel that handles transitions appears.
2. In the Transitions panel, locate the desired transition and choose it from the corresponding category.
3. To align a transition between two clips in the Advanced View timeline, click on the appropriate symbol below and drag it to the cut between the two clips in the panel. After then, let go of the mouse button.

Add a single-sided transition in the Advanced View timeline

When you make a one-sided transition, anything that happens in the Advanced View timeline below shows up in the translucent portion of the transition. For example, to achieve a fade to black, the clip must be on Track 1 or there should be no clips below it. If a clip is on a track above another clip, the lower track's clip will display in the transition, making it seem like the transition is two-sided. **Here are the steps:**

1. On the Action bar of the Advanced View, click **Transitions**. A panel that handles transitions appears.
2. Within the Transitions panel, locate the desired transition and choose it.
3. Pick out a single option:

Please move the transition from the Transitions panel to the edge of the clip if there are no other clips on the same side. To move the transition to the edge of the clip, press and hold the Ctrl key if it is next to another clip.

Apply a default transition in the Advanced View timeline

Here are the steps:
1. **Pick one option from the following:**

Select several clips simultaneously by holding down **Shift** while clicking on them. To choose several clips at once, open the **Project Assets panel**, clicks, and then drag a marquee around the clips you want to use. To select all of the clips, use **Ctrl-A**.

2. When you right-click or control-click on the selected clips, choose **Apply Default Transition along CTI.**
3. **Pick out an option from the list:**
   o Audio
   o Video

For every one of the selected clips, the transition is used.

Using preset transitions over many adjacent clips on the same track:

1. Click the clips with the Ctrl key while holding down the option.
2. Select a clip from the list by right-clicking or using control-clicking.
3. Toggle the Default Transition check box.

At the cut of each successive clip, the transition is applied.

Replace a transition

You can easily replace an existing transition in the timeline of either the Quick View or the Advanced View by dragging a new one on top of it. The alignment and duration of the previous transition are preserved by Premiere Elements when you modify a transition; however, the parameters of the old transition are removed and replaced with the default values of the new transition. **Here are the steps:**

1. Click on **Transitions** in the Quick View or Advanced View's Action bar.
2. From the Transitions menu, choose the transition that will replace the current one.
3. You can move the transition to the appropriate spot in the timeline by dragging it from Quick View or Advanced View.

Preview applied transitions

To see how your transitions will look before you apply them, you may use either the Monitor panel or the contextual control for Transitions. Transitions' contextual control (the letters A and B) allows you to display either default or actual clip thumbnails in the preview area. With the help of the Transitions contextual control, you can see how the transitions will look as you edit them. **Note:** It is possible to see previews in real-time on your TV screen by connecting your digital camcorder to both your computer and TV simultaneously. Now you can notice the shift in the finished film with more clarity.

Preview transitions in the Monitor panel

In either the Quick View or Advanced View timeline, drag the current-time indicator to the left of the transition. Then, press the Play button in the Monitor panel. Keep in mind that you may preview a particular frame of the transition by dragging the current time indication to the right frame in the Monitor panel.

Adjusting transition properties

You can modify the properties of each transition using the contextual control in the Transitions. Common features include things like the border, the anti-aliasing quality setting, the center point's location, and the start and end values. (You may also change the direction of certain transitions.) Below is a summary of the most common controls and choices for changing transition properties. In either the Quick View or the Advanced View timeline, you can access the Transitions contextual control by double-clicking on a transition.

Duration

Determines the transition's duration of time. One second is the default time window.

Alignment

Manages how the clips' transitions are aligned. By default, all clip transitions will be centered.

End/Start Points

Set the beginning and ending points of the transition to determine the percentage of the transition that has been completed.

Display True Sources

Indicates the starting and ending frames of the clips.

Reverse

Reverses the transition. As an example, the Clock Wipe transition is played backward.

Anti-Aligning Quality

Alters the degree to which the transition's edges are smooth.

Custom

Changes parameters that are particular to transitions. Unique parameters are absent from most transitions.

Adjust transition alignment

In either the Quick View or Advanced View timelines, you may use the Transition contextual control to change the alignment of a transition that occurs between two clips. Centering or aligning a transition with a cut is not necessary. Using the drag handle, you may reposition the transition on a cut. The Transition contextual control includes alignment possibilities. Whether or not the clips have been cropped determines how well they can align a transition.

Determine alignment options

See how the pointer changes when placed over a cut in a transition in either Quick View or Advanced View.

- With both clips having their frames cropped at the cut, you have the option to center the transition over the cut or align it on either side of the cut so that it starts or ends at the cut. A clip with an uncut top right corner will have a rounded edge.
- If neither clip contains trimmed frames, the transition will recycle the last frame of the first clip and the first frame of the second clip to fill the transition duration, centering over the cut. (Diagonal bars indicate transitions that use repeated frames.)
- ONLY in cases when the first clip contains clipped frames will the transition automatically go to the beginning of the following clip. There is no duplication of frames in the second clip; instead, the transition makes use of the modified frames from the first clip.
- If the second clip is the only one with chopped frames, the transition will snap to the first clips out point. Here, instead of playing back the original footage, the transition utilizes the modified frames from the second clip.

Adjust alignment for a transition

After selecting the transition in either the Quick View or Advanced View timelines, you can do one of these steps:
- Make sure you can see the current time indicator clearly by placing it above the transition and then zooming in. You can easily reposition the transition by dragging it across the cut.
- By double-clicking the Transition contextual control, you can adjust the transition using its parameters.

Adjust transition duration

You can adjust the duration of a transition by dragging its endpoint in the Quick view or Advanced view timelines. In addition, the Transition contextual control allows you to change the length of a transition. **Here are the steps:**
Pick the transition and then select one of these options from the timelines in Quick View or Advanced View:
- To see the **Trim In** or **Trim Out** indication, hover the mouse over the end of the transition. Press and hold the Trim In or Trim Out icon to adjust the duration.
- Press and hold the transition twice to get the contextual control that allows you to change how long it lasts.

To make a transition longer, either the first or second clip must include enough chopped frames to accommodate the extra time.

Set a default duration for transitions

At startup, the length for both audio and video transitions is set to 30 frames. To make it work better with your movies, you may alter the default duration. Even if the new option doesn't affect any transitions that were already added to the video, all future transitions you put will use this value by default.

1. Select **Edit > Preferences > General or Adobe Premiere Elements 11 > Preferences > General**.
2. After making your selection, click **OK** to save your changes to the default duration for audio or video transitions.

Adjust the center point of a transition

Here are the steps:
1. Click the **transition** twice on the timeline in Quick View or Advanced View.
2. In the contextual control for Transitions, click **More**.
3. To reposition the transition's center, just drag the preview window's little circle. (You can't alter the middle point of every transition.)

Copy and paste transitions in the Advanced View timeline

Select the transition you want to copy and paste, and then select the clips that follow it that have a transition.
1. Select the clips that follow one another and have a transition applied to them.
2. Select the transition you want to use, and then either hit **Ctrl-C** or go to **Edit > Copy.**
3. Choose the clips that will follow this one and apply the duplicated transition to them.
4. Choose either **Edit > Paste** or **Ctrl-V.**

Adding Transitions between video clips and Guided Edits

With their help, the transition between the two videos is more seamless. **Follow these steps in this Guided edit to create seamless transitions between different parts of your video:**
1. The first step in this guided edit is creating transitions between video pieces. To advance or revert through the phases of the guided edit, click **Next and Back.**
2. Press the "**Add media**" button to bring in the video file you want to modify. Disregard the video clip if it is already in the timeline.
3. Determine whether to import media.
4. Select **Guided > Adding Transitions between Video Clips.**
5. Select **Transitions** in the action bar.
6. Be sure to check out all of the possible transitions. To move a transition between videos, just click and drag it.
7. Using the Transitions Adjustments, you can change the playback settings of the transition. Pick an alignment and give it a duration for the transition.

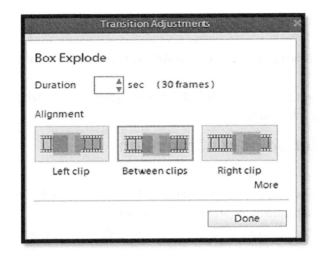

Create an Image Mask Transition

A bitmap picture in black and white can be used as a transition mask. The first clip swaps out the black parts of the picture, while the second clip swaps out the white parts. If you use a grayscale picture as the mask, pixels with a gray value of 50% or more turn into black, and those with a gray value of less than 50% turn into white.

Apply an Image Mask transition

1. On the Action bar of the Advanced View, click **Transitions**.
2. Find the **Image Mask transition** in the Transitions panel's Special Effects section.
3. On the timeline of the Advanced View, drag the Image Mask transition to a cut between clips.
4. The Image Mask Settings dialog box will appear; click on **Select Image.**
5. Just click the "**Open**" button after selecting the image file you want to utilize as a transition mask. This picture is seen in the Picture Mask Settings window.
6. Select **OK** to bring up the contextual control panel for Transitions. Before clicking **Done**, make any necessary changes to the transition's properties.

Change the image for an Image Mask transition

1. On the timeline of the Advanced View, double-click the transition.
2. To access the Transitions contextual control, go to **More** and then choose **Custom**. The image mask settings are shown in a dialog box.
3. For the Image Mask Options dialog box, click **Select Image.**

4. Pick the image file you want to use, open it by clicking the Open button, and then click the OK button.

Create a Gradient Wipe transition

Adobe Premiere Elements allows you to utilize any grayscale image that you can import as a gradient wipe. After filling the black gap with the second clip using a gradient wipe, the grayscale picture moves through each grayscale level until the white space is made transparent. Constructing a Gradient Wipe transition allows you to adjust the degree to which the edges of the transition are rounded off.

Apply a Gradient Wipe transition

1. On the Action bar of the Advanced View, click **Transitions**.
2. Under the Wipe option in the Transitions panel, you should see the **Gradient Wipe transition.**
3. To move the **Gradient Wipe transition** to a specific point between clips, you can use the Advanced View timeline.
4. Once you're in the Gradient Wipe Settings window, click **Select Image**.
5. Click Open after locating and selecting the image file you want to use as the transition. Pictured here is the Gradient Wipe Settings dialogue window.
6. To adjust the suppleness of the transition's edges, use the **Softness** slider. As you drag the slider to the right, the first clip begins to partially cover the second clip. Click on **OK**.
7. Click **Done** after making the necessary changes to the transition's properties using the Transitions contextual control.

Change the image for a Gradient Wipe transition

Here are the steps:
1. In the timeline of the Advanced View, double-click the transition.
2. To access the Transitions contextual control, go to More and then choose Custom. The settings for the gradient wipe appear in a pop-up window.
3. Once you're in the Gradient Wipe Settings window, click **Select Image**.
4. Pick the image file you want to use, open it by clicking the Open button, and then click the **OK** button.

Create a Luma Fade Transition Effect

Use this guided edit to gracefully transition between two media files, whether that's a video and an image or a photo and a video. You can use this guided edit to capture a frame from any source and then modify it using the gradient wipe transition effect. This effect is transferred to the new medium when one is switched.

To use this guided edit, follow these steps:

1. In the **Guided** menu, under **Video Adjustments**, locate **Luma Fade Transition Effect** and choose it.
2. Press "**Add media**" to bring in two videos, two photos, or a video and an image for editing.
3. Select the appropriate media import option.
4. To choose both files, press and hold the **Shift** key. Place the content on Track 1 at the point when the timeline shows the current time indicator (CTI). Before going on to Step 5, make sure the CTI is moved to the end of the first clip or photo. In guided mode, the CTI will automatically go to the conclusion of the first media.
5. To capture a still image from the video, use the **Freeze Frame button.**

6. Click Export and choose a place in the Freeze Frame dialog box to export a frame as a picture to the location of your choice.
7. Select the **Transition** icon on the right side of the panel. From the Transitions panel, drag the **Gradient Wipe transition** to the selected area of the timeline near CTI.
8. Click **Select Image** on the Gradient Wipe Settings dialog box to choose the image you saved using the Freeze Frame dialog box. Choose **OK**.
9. **The following steps will guide you through the Transition Adjustments dialog box to modify the transition properties:**
   ○ Enter the duration in seconds for the transition between the two formats. The default is **one second.**
   ○ Choose **Between clips** for the alignment by clicking **More.**
   ○ Click **Apply** to put the adjustments into effect.
10. You can see the outcomes by selecting "**Play**".

CHAPTER 9
KEYFRAMES AND ADVANCED MOTION CONTROL

Introduction to Keyframes

When editing videos, keyframes are a must-have for creating seamless transitions, animations, and effects that evolve. Keyframes are fundamental to creating a dynamic video, whether you want to change the size of an item, have it move across the screen, or change the level of the music. Using keyframes, a user may easily include dynamic changes in their work in Adobe Premiere Elements without resorting to complex technologies. The most basic definition of a keyframe is the instant in time at which an element's attribute is changed. To have an object begin at a certain place in a clip, you may put a keyframe at the beginning and then add another keyframe to change its position later on. To make the animation flow smoothly, the program fills in the gaps between the keyframes. Interpolation is the magic ingredient that gives video editing that polished, expert look and feel. Even anyone unfamiliar with video editing will find Adobe Premiere Elements' keyframes user-friendly. Using keyframes, you may modify elements' attributes like as opacity, audio levels, motion, and special effects in Premiere Elements. Putting a keyframe at the beginning of the clip with the original size and another keyframe later on with the zoomed-in size is one way to get a progressive zoom-in effect on an image. Premiere Elements will take care of the transition between the two spots, giving the illusion of a progressive zoom.

Premiere Elements' visual cues for keyframes are one of its user-friendly features. You can easily keep track of your edits and make any necessary tweaks by seeing the placement of keyframes on the timeline. When it comes to perfecting animations or making sure transitions occur at the perfect time, this visual input is crucial. Adobe Premiere Elements makes adding keyframes a breeze. To begin animating, choose the clip you want to change, then click the stopwatch symbol next to the effect or attribute you wish to change. You may add a keyframe at the location of your playhead by doing this. Altering the property at one point in the timeline will trigger the creation of a new keyframe at the next point in the timeline. Because of this adaptability, you can make more interesting movies with less effort and experiment with various effects. Audio adjustments may also be made using keyframes. One useful feature is the ability to use keyframes to control the level, which allows for seamless transitions between different types of audio, such as background music and conversation. With this much flexibility, you may make tweaks to the audio that sound professional and you won't even need dedicated audio software. In conclusion, Adobe Premiere Elements' keyframes provide you the freedom to express yourself creatively and dynamically in your video productions.

With their help, you can add eye-catching animations and transitions to your material, taking it to the next level of engagement. Keyframes are a great tool for improving video quality and gaining confidence to explore more sophisticated editing methods. Even if you're just starting, practicing with them will help you succeed.

Applying Motion Keyframes to Create Dynamic Effects

Keyframing and Animation

Premiere Elements' keyframes and animation provide powerful tools for users to create visually appealing and dynamic movies. Using these capabilities to provide various project pieces of motion might enhance the overall movie experience. At certain points in time, known as "**keyframes**," Premiere Elements allows you to modify the location, size, and transparency of an effect or feature. Altering these keyframes over time allows you to create intricate and smooth pictures. We add motion to a clip using keyframes. The location or impact of a clip might determine this movement. Adding keyframes to a keyframe sequence allows us to examine or manipulate an object. Let's begin by animating a clip. It's not easy to describe, yet doing it is child's play.

Animating clips

Two clips that are overlaid are used in this example. At the bottom, you can see the cloudy background; at the top, you can see Superman. The Superman clip employed the "**Chroma**" technique to make the backdrop see-through. It gives the impression that Superman is soaring through the sky.

Superman is now a dot in the sky, like a hummingbird, so I animated him to fly across the screen from right to left.

- I started by selecting the Superman clip from the Timeline after placing the time marker in the first frame.
- Hover over the "**Edit**" tab, and then choose the "**Filters**" menu item.
- At the very base of the Effects window, you should see the "**Editing Effects**" button; click on it.
- The panel for editing effects opens up when you do this.
- After selecting "**Motion**," click "**Show Keyframes**."

- To insert keyframes, next to the "**Motion**" effect, click the "**Toggle the effect on or off**" button. Why was this added to the "**Motion**" effect? Because we could move Superman around the screen.

To apply the "**Motion**" effect, what steps are necessary?

Let's go.

- You can also find a time display and a calendar in the "**Keyframes**" window, as seen in the image below.
- You can reposition them by clicking and dragging and you can also change the position of the Time sign that appears above the Timeline. This sign is identical; it just functions in two distinct locations. I want you to grasp and keep this in mind.
- If I click the "**Toggle the effect on or off**" button, a primary frame will be added to the first frame of the clip.

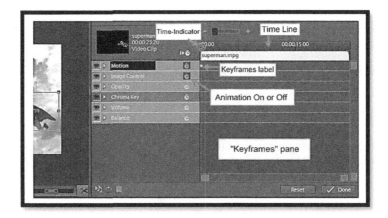

- To move Superman from one frame to the next, place the first-time sign in the timeline's final frame (1)
- Move **Superman** to the left side of the screen by clicking on him (2).
- This complements the "**Motion**" effect in the Superman clip by itself by adding a keyframe to the last frame (3).
- It's the reason why the screen moves (4).
- When I play back the rendered video by pressing the **Enter** key, we can see Superman's right-to-left movement across the screen.

Working with Scaling, Rotation, and Positioning

The Motion effect is automatically added to every clip in the Quick view timeline and the Advanced view timeline. To move, rotate, or resize an image inside the video frame, you may apply the Motion effect. The Motion effect is another option for establishing the starting point. By default, the anchor point—which is often located in the middle of the clip—is used to determine the values of position, scale, and rotation? Because of their spatial nature, the Position, Scale, and Rotation characteristics are best adjusted via the Monitor panel.

Note: Please be aware that to animate clips, you must first establish keyframes for the Motion attributes.

Adjust a clip's position

1. Choose the video from either the Quick View or the Advanced View timeline.
2. To move the clip, use the mouse to drag it in the Monitor panel; be careful not to drag any handles.

Note: You can create keyframes as you work with the clip in the Monitor panel to make it move over time.

Scale a clip

1. Choose the video from either the Quick View or the Advanced View timeline.
2. Click the **Applied Effects** button.
3. **Do any of the following:**

Drag a clip handle in the Monitor panel to resize proportionately. Just click and hold the clip. Second, you may open the Applied Effects panel, expand the Motion effect, and then adjust the Scale slider. Drag any clip handle in the Monitor panel to independently scale height and width. It's also possible to expand the Motion effect in the Applied Effects panel and uncheck Constrain Proportions. The other option is to open the Applied Effects panel, expand the Motion effect, and then adjust the Scale Height and Scale Width sliders.

Note: If you scale low-resolution photos or videos to 100%, they could seem pixelated or blocky. To avoid pixelation, Premiere Elements rasterizes scaled EPS files continually.

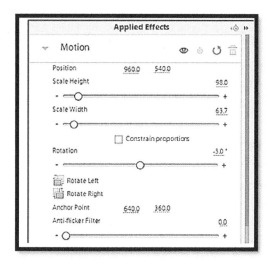

Applied Effects panel with the Motion effect selected, and the Monitor panel with a clip handle selected for scaling.

Use a clip at its original size

Premiere Elements automatically resizes any clips you import to match the dimensions of your project. Do this if you'd want to utilize a clip at its original size:

1. In the **Project Assets** panel, find the clip and click on it.
2. Tap on **Clip** and then choose **Video Options**.
3. Deselect **Scale To Frame Size.**

Rotate a clip

1. Choose the video from either the Quick View or the Advanced View timeline.
2. Click the **Applied Effects** button.
3. In the Applied Effects panel, expand the Motion effect and then perform one of these things:
- Find the underlined value and move it to the right of Rotation.
- For a full 360-degree spin, choose Rotate Left or Rotate Right.

Adjust a clip's anchor point

1. Choose the video from either the Quick View or the Advanced View timeline.
2. Click the **Applied Effects** button.
3. The Applied Effects panel is where you can expand the Motion effect.
4. The Motion effect's anchor point sliders can be dragged.

Adding Keyframes for Text and Graphic Animations

You can give your video projects a lively and interesting twist by animating text and images in Adobe Premiere Elements. Keyframes are essential for animating the movement, change, or fading of these components. To make animations that glide along, keyframes are used to control attributes like position, scale, and opacity. In Premiere Elements, you can animate text and graphics using keyframes:

Step-by-Step Guide to Adding Keyframes

1. **Select Your Text or Graphic Clip**: To begin animating, go to the timeline and choose the piece of text or image you want to use. To access the element's attributes, click on it to highlight it.
2. **Open the Applied Effects Panel**: Access the "Applied Effects" panel by going to the panel on the right side of your screen. To make it visible, choose "Applied Effects" from the "Window" menu if it isn't already.
3. **Choose the Property to Animate**: In the Applied Effects panel, find the property you want to animate. You may choose Position, Scale, or Opacity, for example, to have the element move, resize, or fade in or out. Be careful to add the effect to the element before you apply it.
4. **Activate Keyframing**: To enable keyframing, locate the property you want to animate and click on its stopwatch symbol. This will add your first keyframe at the current location of the playhead, indicating the beginning of the animation.

5. **Set the Initial Keyframe**: Make the necessary adjustments to the property to set the first keyframe to the value you choose. To have the text or picture appear off-screen at the beginning of an animated slide-in effect, for instance, you would need to adjust the starting position.
6. **Move the Playhead to a New Position**: You may modify the start or finish point of the animation by dragging the playhead to a different location in the timeline.
7. **Add the Next Keyframe**: After you've added the next keyframe, you may change the property to the final value you want. You may make the text glide in by dragging it to the middle of the frame, for example. A new keyframe will be added automatically at this location by Premiere Elements.
8. **Preview Your Animation**: You may preview your animation by playing back the timeline and looking at the transition from the first keyframe to the second. To fine-tune the animation, move and change the value of keyframes as necessary.

Common Animation Examples

- **Sliding Text or Graphics**: Start by inserting a keyframe at the beginning of your project with the Position attribute set to off-screen. This will make the title glide in from the left. Just a few seconds after the title reaches its last on-screen position, set another keyframe.
- **Fading In and Out**: To get a fade-in effect, first set a keyframe with 0% opacity. Then, at the time when you want the text to be completely visible, put a second keyframe with 100% opacity. To achieve a fade-out, insert one more keyframe with an opacity of 100% and one more with 0% just before the clip concludes.

Tips for Smooth Animations

- **Ease In/Out**: Use ease-in and ease-out effects to make the animation seem more natural. Instead of stopping suddenly, the movement will begin or finish more gently using this.
- **Adjust Timing**: Move the keyframes closer or further apart on the timeline to alter the pace of the animation if it seems too sluggish or quick.

Advanced Keyframe Editing

Moving and adjusting keyframes by hand on the timeline gives you greater control. You may adjust the timing of keyframes by clicking and dragging them, or you can delete or copy them using the right-click menu. Making animations with various modifications may be made easier using this.

Tips for Smooth Motion and Consistency

Your animations and video cuts will seem more polished and interesting if you can get the motion to flow smoothly and stay consistent. Here are some helpful hints for using Adobe Premiere Elements to make animations that flow smoothly and appear consistent:

1. **Use Ease In and Ease Out**

Using the Ease In and Ease Out settings may greatly improve the quality of keyframe animations. With these parameters, your animations may begin and stop more subtly, creating the illusion of a more organic flow. The lack of these features might cause animations to seem robotic or abrupt. Select the ease option you want to use by right-clicking on a keyframe in the timeline.

2. **Keep Timing Consistent**

Maintaining a steady beat will make sure that your animations don't seem out of sync. Try to maintain consistent timing if you're doing many identical animations (such as text sliding in for various portions). If, for example, the duration of the initial text animation is two seconds, then any subsequent animations of a similar kind should be two seconds long as well. This maintains a consistent tempo and makes for a more unified viewing experience.

3. **Adjust Keyframe Spacing**

The animation will go more quickly if the keyframes are near together and more slowly if they are further apart. Consider using uniform keyframe spacing and making any required adjustments when attempting to generate smooth motion. To produce a more gradual shift and slow down the animation if it seems too abrupt, slide the keyframes farther apart.

4. **Use Motion Blur (If Available)**

Even while Adobe Premiere Elements doesn't have motion blur built in like other more powerful programs, you may make it seem like it does by applying a little blur effect when the action is happening quickly. This lessens the jagged appearance that might result from fast motions and helps to give the illusion of spontaneous motion.

5. **Check Playback Regularly**

Make sure your animation is flowing as planned by playing it again at regular intervals. You may easily find any unexpected leaps or irregularities in the motion that may need correcting by previewing your adjustments. If you need to inspect animations frame-by-frame to detect minor problems, you may do so using the playback settings.

6. **Align Motion Paths Smoothly**

Verify that the motion route of animated objects moving across the screen is smooth and makes sense. Animations could seem clumsy if their trajectories are jagged or irregular. To fine-tune the trajectory or orientation of a motion, just click and drag the handles on the route. This is of utmost importance in intricate animations involving elements that traverse paths that include curves or several twists.

7. **Maintain Consistent Properties**

Make sure that characteristics like opacity, rotation, and scale remain constant while animating several components in a project. If an animation has a graphic that scales from 100% to 120%, for instance, it would be visually inconsistent if other visuals did not utilize the same range.

8. **Use Guides and Grids**

You may use the grids and guidelines in Adobe Premiere components to make sure that all of your animated components stay in place. You may use this to make sure that the text and visuals are aligned or spaced evenly. You can keep your project looking professional by making sure your animations are aligned.

9. **Avoid Overusing Effects**

Although it's tempting to add effects and transitions to animations, doing so too often might result in chaotic and uncoordinated looks. Keep things simple and add effects only if they improve the content. That way, the audience won't be distracted and can concentrate on your tale or message.

10. **Practice and Refine**

Finally, mastering the art of keyframe and effect animation will allow you to create motion that is both smooth and consistent. Try out various configurations, study up on tutorials, and make mental notes of any animations that catch your eye. Improving your initiatives over time is possible with the use of these ideas.

CHAPTER 10
CREATE A VIDEO STORY OR VIDEO COLLAGE

As well as being a creative means of preserving and sharing memories, collages can tell a story. In this guide, you'll find the steps to make your video collage and how to customize it. Although picture collages have always been the most popular kind of work, Premiere Elements now also lets you make video collages. However, it's not limited to video memories; you can also mix and match photos and videos to create engaging and interactive video collages. By picking out a template from the offered options, you can easily put together a memory book and share it with loved ones.

Create a video collage

Here are the steps:

1. Make your video collage using one of these methods:

Premiere Elements' Video Collage function can be accessed via the Create menu. The next step is to choose the media files you want to use for the collage.

2. Use the drop-down option to choose a pre-made format. The number of grids and the effects applied to those grids are two of the many unique aspects of each template. Some examples of available designs include three-grid layouts with the Slide In effect, while others have five-grid layouts with the Rotate effect.
3. The Media bin is where you should save any media files that you want to include in your video collage. Images and videos may be imported from your computer's hard drive or the Elements Organizer.

Files and folders: Importing media from your computer's hard drive requires you to choose certain files and folders.

4. Simply drag and drop media files from the Media library into the collage. It is possible to preview media assets in the Media bin before adding them to the collage. Also, the organizer lets you drag and drop media files into the college.
5. Make the movie collage exactly as you want it by adjusting the contextual parameters. It is important to keep in mind that the pan and zoom effect is automatically applied to pictures.

Customize video collage

Resize handles

You can adjust the grid size and media type with the simple slide of a handle.

Move and Pan Tool

- To reposition the media inside the grid, just use the mouse cursor on the "**Pan**" tool.
- Click outside the pan tool's window and drag the selection to shift the grid and its contents.

Zoom slider

By dragging the slider to the left, you can zoom out, and by dragging it to the right, you can zoom in.

Delete

Eliminate the grid and all the media. Keep in mind that erasing the grid will prevent you from adding it again. But you can undo the removal and put the grid back together if you want to.

Swap Media

If you could switch out the media in the present grid with the media in the other grids, that would be great. Select the desired grid, and then hit the **Swap Media button** to change the media. Once you're ready to change out some material, just drag it on the grid. The option to cut the edited video has also been changed. Simply drag the media file from the media bin onto the grid to replace the current media file on the grid with the one in the media bin.

Trim Media (Video only)

Cut the footage to the desired length or choose individual frames from the tape to use in your movie.

Mute/Unmute clip audio (Video only)

In the current grid, you can choose to muffle or unmute the audio of the clip.

Video Collage settings

Templates

Swap out the original video collage template with one of these alternatives. Either double-click a template to open it in a new window, or choose one from the drop-down menu and then hit the **Apply** button to make changes.

Playback Settings

The collage can only be played back when the playback settings have been set.

Play each piece of media one after the other

Add music

By navigating to the music library in Premiere Elements, you have the option to include background music in your collage. You may either double-click on a music score to add it or pick it and then click the **Apply button** to add it. You may remove the background music from your video collage by selecting **No Background Music** from the options.

Preview video collage

- Get a preview of your video collage with the touch of ⊙ button.
- Press the **Render button** to make sure the playback goes smoothly.
- Keep in mind that it can take a while for the preview of your video collage to load entirely.

Save and export video collage

Save a Video Collage Project

One of the following actions must be taken to preserve a video collage:
- Find the **Save button** on the Taskbar and click on it.
- Click on "**Save**" in the **File** menu.

When you save the Video Collage Project to your PC, the filename extension is .vc. Just a heads up, the identical location will also generate a file with the .vct extension. This file is required to access the video collage. Avoid erasing this file at any cost.

Open a Video Collage Project

Launching a video collage project requires doing one of the following:
- Select **File > Open Project** from the drop-down menu in the Premiere Elements workspace.
- Select "**Open Video Project**" from the **File** menu inside the Video Collage workspace.
- After you locate the file with the extension .vc, click on the **Open** button.

Note: Don't save a file called placeholder.png to the same folder as your video collage. The Video Collage workspace will not load properly and an error notice indicating that the media is unavailable will be shown if you do this.

Export a Video Collage

Afterward, you should showcase your video collage once you have completed all of the editing. You can export and share your video collage in a few different ways.

Export to timeline

After you've finished editing your video collage, you can save it to your timeline by clicking the Export to timeline option. Before sharing your college with others, you may use this option to make changes and revisions.

Export and Share

All of the available export formats are consolidated into one screen by selecting the Export & Share option. The Export & Share panel categorizes the many exportable and shareable files into their respective tabs. An assortment of devices, such as laptops, mobile phones, and the web, may see your video collage if you want to export it. Take note that you can't export a video collage on a CD, save it as an audio file, or save it as a picture file. Your video collage can still be exported to a timeline, and then you may burn a DVD by choosing the Export & Share option from the menu.

Video Collage project settings

When you use Video Collage, you have the option to save your compositions in either 4K or HD resolution. Any of the project settings can be used to construct a video collage; however, to get **the desired results on the timeline, you need to either start with a blank timeline or adhere to these steps:**

1. Choose a resolution of **1920 x 1080 or 4K** when you start a new project.
2. You can make all the changes you want to the video collage after you've made it before exporting it to the timeline.
3. If you start a video collage project without a timeline, the project settings will be automatically adjusted to accommodate an HD or 4K video collage.

CHAPTER 11

SPECIAL EFFECTS AND CREATIVE ENHANCEMENTS

Creating Green Screen Effects (Chroma Key)

The ability to change the scene or background of a video by removing a solid-color background (usually green) is known as a green screen effect or chroma keying. This method is well-liked because it gives users greater freedom to express themselves creatively while making films that seem professional. With just a few clicks in Adobe Premiere Elements, you can add green screen effects to your videos. **The way to accomplish it is this:**

1. **Import Your Footage**

Bring in both the green screen and the new backdrop (picture or video clip) for the video. Click the Add Media option, Select the source (such as your PC), and then choose the files you want to import. Using the Advanced View, drag and drop these clips into your timeline.

2. **Place Your Clips on the Timeline**

A track should be placed atop the backdrop clip to hold the green screen video. Put the green screen film on Video Track 2, for instance, if you're using Video Track 1 for your backdrop picture or video. When the green is gone, the backdrop will still be visible because of the layering.

3. **Apply the Chroma Key Effect**

To access the Effects panel, locate your green screen clip in the timeline and click on it. Just put "Chroma Key" into the search box to get the effect. Place the Chroma Key effect on top of your green screen footage by dragging and dropping.

4. **Adjust the Chroma Key Settings**

Go to the Applied Effects section and tweak the parameters while keeping your green screen clip selected. The Chroma Key effect's settings are located here:

- **Key Color**: To choose the green background as your video's key color, click on it using the eyedropper tool. This instructs Premiere Elements to eliminate a certain hue.
- **Tolerance**: You may use this slider to control the amount of green that is eliminated. To eliminate additional shades of green, increase the tolerance; however, be cautious not to remove any elements of your subject.
- **Edge Feather**: This makes the cutout seem less sharp and more organic by feathering its edges.
- **Opacity**: To keep the topic completely visible, set the opacity to 100%.

5. **Refine the Effect**

Make sure the backdrop is fully erased and your subject is neatly cropped by adjusting the parameters. Make sure your topic is free of artifacts and sharp edges by adjusting the tolerance and feathering.

6. **Preview Your Result**

To preview the new backdrop effect with the green screen, play back your timeline. Verify that the subject disappears into the backdrop without a trace and that no trace of green remains.

7. **Add Additional Adjustments (Optional)**

Effects like color correction and brightness tweaks may help bring the subject and background lighting into harmony, which in turn improves the final product. A more unified and lifelike appearance may be achieved with this.

8. **Export Your Video**

When you're happy with the green screen effect, go to **File > Export & Share** to save your video. Select the format and quality options that are most suited to your project.

Tips for Best Results

- **Use Good Lighting**: Make sure the green screen is well-lit and free of shadows by following these lighting guidelines. Because of this, removing the backdrop in Premiere Elements is a breeze.
- **Avoid Clothing That Matches the Background**: Make sure your subject isn't wearing colors that match the green screen to avoid having sections of them deleted.
- **High-Quality Footage**: Higher-resolution film helps save details and gives the impression of greater professionalism, thus it's important to use it.

Using Slow Motion and Time-Lapse

Your video may gain visual appeal and energy by using time-lapse or slow-motion effects. You may accentuate moments or compress extensive sequences into shorter, more compelling segments with the help of Adobe Premiere Elements' simple tools for creating these effects. Premiere Elements's slow-motion and time-lapse features are explained here.

Creating Slow Motion

1. **Import Your Video Clip**: To begin slowing down a video, import the clip you want to use. Select your clip's source—your PC or a linked device—under Add Media. When the clip is imported, just drop it into the timeline.
2. **Select the Clip**: To choose a clip, just click on it in the timeline. Doing so will make available clip-specific editing tools.
3. **Apply the Time Stretch Tool**: To use the Time Stretch Tool, choose the clip you want to edit, then right-click on it and select Time Stretch from the menu that appears. You may manually change the clip's speed using this tool. A dialog window showing the speed in percentage form will pop up.

4. **Adjust the Speed**: The speed may be adjusted to produce a slow-motion effect. For example, if you set the speed to 50%, the clip will play at half its original pace. Slower motion is achieved with smaller percentages. Before you commit, check the preview to make sure the effect fits your needs.

5. **Smooth the Motion (Optional)**: Use the Frame Blending option in the Applied Effects tab to smooth out any jerky movements in the slow-motion effect. Improved frame-to-frame transitions are a result of this.

6. **Preview and Fine-Tune**: You may preview and fine-tune the footage by playing it back in the timeline. If you need to, you may adjust the speed even more until you get the effect you want.

Creating a Time-Lapse

1. **Import the Sequence of Photos or Video**: A time-lapse may be created using a lengthy video clip or a sequence of still images. Simply import the photographs in order by navigating to the Add Media menu and choosing your images. Make sure to number them consecutively. You might also just drag the clip you want to accelerate onto the timeline.

2. **Set the Duration for Photos (Photo Sequence Only)**: Time Stretch or adjusting the duration in the Properties panel are two ways to set the length for photographs. To do this, select all of the photos in the timeline and right-click. To provide the impression of rapid movement, choose a shorter length for each shot (e.g., 0.1 seconds).

3. **Adjust Speed for Video Clips**: Pick the video clip you want to use as a time-lapse, then right-click on it and pick Time Stretch from the menu that appears. To get a time-lapse effect, try increasing the speed percentage to 500% or higher, which is higher than 100%. Long sequences will play back more quickly because of this compression.

4. **Preview Your Time-Lapse**: You may get a preview of your time-lapse in action by looking at the timeline. To get a polished and aesthetically pleasing outcome, tweak the speed parameters as necessary.

CHAPTER 12
WORKING WITH VIDEO FORMATS AND EXPORTING

Understanding File Formats and Codecs

If you want your finished videos to look great and perform flawlessly on all devices, you need to know your way around file types and codecs in video editing software like Adobe Premiere Elements. The following is an explanation of the many file types and codecs, how they function, and why they are important in the world of video editing.

What Are File Formats?

Video, audio, and other types of data are stored in file formats. Some of the most used formats for video files include **MP4, MOV, AVI, and MKV**. Codecs are necessary because file formats specify the storage and media types that may be included inside them, but they do not specify the compression or encoding methods.

What Are Codecs?

Software or hardware tools that can compress and decompress audio and video data are known as **codecs**, an abbreviation for **coder-decoder.** With the use of codecs, huge video files may be compressed to smaller ones without sacrificing quality, making them easier to store and view. To make video storage and playback more efficient, codecs compress data before exporting or playing the file. **Here are some commonly used video codecs:**

- **H.264**: Because of its capacity to reduce video file sizes without sacrificing quality, H.264 has become one of the most widely used codecs. It's compatible with a large variety of devices and systems.
- **HEVC (H.265)**: A more recent codec, HEVC (H.265) provides superior compression than H.264 without sacrificing quality. Encoding and decoding it may need more computing power, but it's perfect for 4K and other high-resolution media.
- **ProRes**: Apple's high-quality codec that keeps video quality when edited, although it makes files bigger. It is often used in workflows for professional editing.
- **AVI (Audio Video Interleave)**: Older formats like AVI (Audio Video Interleave) may handle more codecs but aren't as efficient as more recent ones like MP4.

How File Formats and Codecs Work Together

The codec reduces the data's size inside the file format, which stores the video, audio, and other data. To compress videos, for instance, the MP4 file format is compatible with the H.264 codec. To export or edit video in Adobe Premiere Elements in a way that is compatible with the desired platform retains the quality, and plays back smoothly, you need to choose the correct combination of file format and codec.

Common Video File Formats and Their Uses

- **MP4**: When it comes to sharing videos online and on different devices, MP4 is by far the most popular format. The H.264 codec is often used, and it provides an acceptable trade-off between quality and file size.
- **MOV**: MOV is an Apple-created format that is often used with the ProRes codec for professional-grade editing. Although it might be greater in size, it is usually employed in professional situations.
- **AVI**: A more traditional format that works with more codecs but has a higher file size and isn't as device-specific as MP4.
- **MKV (Matroska)**: A versatile format that supports an endless amount of audio, video, and subtitle tracks. Though not all devices will be able to use it without installing extra software, it is popular for high-quality films.

Choosing the Right Format and Codec in Premiere Elements

If you're looking to export your films in a variety of formats and codecs, Adobe Premiere Elements has you covered. **Here are some things to think about when choosing a codec and format:**

1. **Purpose of the Video**: The H.264 codec is often the way to choose when making videos to share online or on social media. It's compatible with a lot of platforms and keeps the file size and quality in check. Formats like MOV with the ProRes codec are good options for professional editing or long-term archiving.
2. **Compatibility**: Please check the format's and codec's compatibility with the platform or device you want to use. For example, H.264 is a solid option for the majority of video productions because of its compatibility with popular platforms like Vimeo, YouTube, and social media.
3. **File Size and Quality**: Consider the trade-offs between file size and quality before making your final decision. For professional editing, a codec like ProRes will provide larger files with greater quality. In contrast, H.264 is superior for smaller files without sacrificing quality.

Understanding Bitrate

When discussing codecs and formats, bitrate is an additional critical component. Kilobits per second (kbps) or megabits per second (Mbps) are common units of measurement for the data processing rate. In most cases, a greater bitrate will result in higher-quality video but also bigger file sizes. Premiere Elements' bitrate adjustment allows users to achieve a happy medium between file size and quality while exporting.

Export and share your videos

Sharing Center has made sharing your films easier and more streamlined than ever. **Quick Export** allows you to export your projects at a quicker rate. Alternatively, you can find all the necessary tools to save and share your completed project in the **Export & Share** tab. Many devices, including PCs, mobile phones, and the web, may play videos that you've saved. A consolidated panel displaying all export formats is provided by the **Export & Share** option. The many media possibilities are represented by individual tabs on the **Export & Share** panel.

Quick Export

The quickest method to export videos is using the **Quick Export** option. Any device should be able to play back videos made using **Quick Export.** Several web-based services also allow you to share this format. To export your movie, you need to enter the location where you want to store it, choose a preset from the menu, and then hit the **Export** button.

Computer

Once you're done editing a movie in either **Quick View or Advanced View**, you can export or share the file as its standalone video file. As soon as you export, you can open it in any media player or editing tool on your computer, or transfer it to another computer. Thanks to Premiere Elements' built-in optimizations for various mobile devices, you can easily export your video in a format that works on any of them. For optimal results, you may stick with the default settings.

1. Pick out the files you want to export.
2. To access the **Export** workspace in Premiere Elements, go to the top header bar and choose **Export & Share**.

A left-to-right movement characterizes the export process. First, choose an option from the left-hand column to save your movie to: YouTube, Vimeo, Facebook, Instagram, Pinterest, LinkedIn, or Your Local Computer. Depending on your destination, Premiere Elements will provide you with the best export options.

3. Either use the Preset menu to choose a new H.264 preset or accept the default one. In addition to the Preset drop-down menu, the dotted menu allows you to personalize your export parameters and store your own presets.

Note: Please be aware that while you may customize each export parameter to your liking, the Match Source defaults are usually your best bet. These adaptive presets mimic your original in every way, including frame rate, size, and more. To export a video with excellent quality, use the High Bitrate preset.

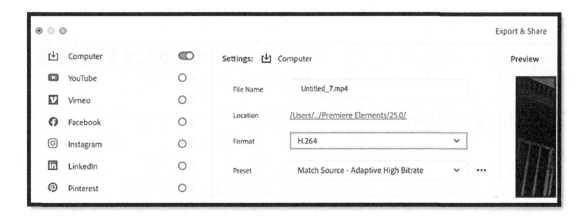

4. In the Preview box, you can see how your material will look before exporting, scrub it, play it back, specify a custom length, and adjust the source video's placement inside the output frame if you're exporting to a different size.
   o **Range** lets you customize the duration of your exported video.
      ▪ **Entire Source**: if the entire duration of the sequence or clip will be exported
      ▪ **Work Area**: exports the Work Area Bar duration (sequences only)
      ▪ **Custom**: honors custom In/Out Points set in Export mode
   o **Scaling** lets you adjust how the source fits within the exported frame when exporting to a different frame size.
      ▪ **Scale to fit**: Resizes the source to fit the output frame without any distortion or cropped pixels. Black bars may be visible.
      ▪ **Scale to fill**: Resizes the source to fill the output frame with no black bars. Some pixels may be cropped.
      ▪ **Stretch to fill**: Stretches the source to fill the output frame without any black bars or cropped pixels. The frame aspect is not maintained so the video may look distorted.
5. Proceed to click **Export**.

Social Media

You can export your movie in formats that are compatible with Internet distribution using Premiere Elements. The Export & Share window allows you to publish your video straight to the web. In the Social Media section, choose a website that allows users to share content. There are several choices, including Vimeo, Facebook, Instagram, LinkedIn, and Pinterest. You can export your video quickly by using the default parameters. Furthermore, the parameters may be adjusted to suit individual needs. But before you upload your film, check that the data rate is compatible with the device you want to play it on. Click **Sign-in** to begin the authorization process for **YouTube**, **Facebook**, and **Vimeo**. Once you're done, you can continue with the sharing procedure of the platform of your choice. Just copy the video to a local folder and then paste it into the chosen platform to post on **Pinterest, LinkedIn, or Instagram.**

Exporting Options
DVD

You can burn your project to DVD using a DVD burner, which can be connected to or installed on your computer. This will allow you to play the project on a standard DVD player. Several pre-made designs are available in Premiere Elements' DVD Layout window that streamlines the creation of interactive DVD menus.

Videotape

You can record your masterpiece onto a DV tape in the same manner you could just record video from one. Here we go again with the familiar IEEE 1394 cable—also called FireWire or iLink—to transfer video and audio from your computer to your camera.

Movie files

There is a gradual expansion of complex export choices when you decide to save a video file. To achieve your goal, you choose the set of choices that works best for you in that situation. What are your plans for displaying the movie online, playing it from a CD-ROM, or incorporating it into another application? Fortunately, Premiere Elements comes with several default options that are tailored to address the most common output requirements.

Still images and audio-only files

Not only can users export the whole edited sequence to DVD or tape, but they also often make use of a few other export choices. It is possible to extract a still picture from any frame of the movie and then export it. In both the Clip view and the Timeline view, you may locate the Monitor window, which is a great spot to locate the Export button. Making a still picture for use as a project freeze frame or printing becomes much easier with this. You may also export an audio-only file. To illustrate the point, consider the possibility of using an interview's audio track only for voiceover purposes. This is because removing the video track from an audio file significantly reduces its file size. Adobe Premiere Elements has built-in tools for rapid video sharing and exporting. The Export & Share tab allows you to store and share your finished films. With Quick Export, you can save all of your videos to one file that works on almost any platform out there. **This includes desktop PCs, laptops, smartphones, and tablets.**

1. Select **Export & Share** from the workspace that is associated with Adobe Premiere Elements.
2. When prompted, choose **Quick Export** from the **Export & Share** dialog box's drop-down option.

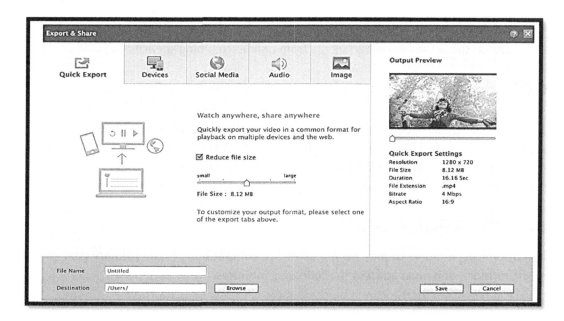

3. (Optional) Choose the decrease File Size checkbox and then make use of the sliders that are located below to compress and decrease the size of your video according to your preferences.
4. Put in the file's name and the directory where you want the output movie saved.
5. Click the **Save** button.

Movie Files and Export Presets

You can export a video file for several uses, such as making it playable on a CD-ROM, sending it over the internet, or importing it into another program. For each distribution channel, there is a wide variety of formats to choose from, sometimes called media architectures. However, the user can customize the movie's crucial attributes—frame size, frame rate, audio quality, etc.— within each architecture's abundance of possibilities. The settings also dictate the specific codec (compression technique) that is used to encode the file. Both the maximum file size and the compatibility with different programs are affected by the codec. Thanks to Premiere Elements, you won't have to learn and specify a plethora of settings to do tasks that would otherwise be a pain. This encompasses the steps required to export a video file. **Premiere Elements offers presets for the following file types:**

- **MPEG—.** Multiple sets of compression standards have been developed by the Moving Picture Advanced Group (MPEG, pronounced "em-peg"). The organization is named after several formats, including MPEG-1 and MPEG-2. (The full name of the widely used MP3 audio format is MPEG-layer 3.)
- **QuickTime—.** Apple systems' multimedia architecture includes a wide variety of codecs designed for usage in various applications.
- **Windows Media**: Windows Media is Microsoft's protocol for low-data-rate applications, such as those that download media from online streaming services.

CODECS

There is a compressor/decompressor called a "codec" in tech. As with "capture" and "rendering," the word "compressor" means "to encode a file." On the other hand, "decompressor" is associated with playback and means to decode a file. Codec refers to a certain technique for compression, an approach to compressing and decompressing files.

EXPORTING FOR CD-ROM

When optimizing a movie to play from a CD-ROM, compatibility is the primary goal you strive for. Furthermore, you must address the following inquiries:

- Is it necessary for the film to be compatible with several platforms?
- When watching the film, what kind of media player will be utilized?
- What is the slowest possible speed for the CD drive that will be utilized to play the movie?
- To make it possible to watch the film on a computer, a copy will be created from the CD. Which slower hard disk will be used to play back the video, if that is the case?
- To what extent do you need a certain degree of picture quality?

- Could you please tell me how much time the movie runs in total and how much smaller the file has to be to fit on a regular CD-ROM?

EXPORTING FOR THE WEB

The file size (and its related twin, the data rate) is the most critical factor to optimize for online movie distribution. If you want to watch a movie online, you should set the movie's data rate to the lowest possible speed that you can tolerate. Despite lightning-fast connections, this remains a major limitation. A choice must be made as to whether the fast playback capability is valuable enough to warrant the loss of quality. There are often many fewer limits when it comes to downloadable movies. In this case, the file size determines how long your viewers will have to wait to see your movie. Assuming the viewer uses a progressive download method, the file size remains an issue even after the video begins playing. If the film goes on for more than, say, a minute, this becomes even more apparent.

EXPORT FOR OTHER PROGRAMS

What you need to think about when exporting video from Premiere Elements to use in another application differs based on the format and the program you're obtaining it from. But there are several common worries that you should be aware of. You should be well-versed in the file formats and compression methods supported by the program. Select a codec that supports alpha channels when exporting to QuickTime. For example, Uncompressed in Windows Media or None in Animation are good options. You may maintain the video's transparency in this way. Be aware that the video's resolution reduces to 72 dots per inch when exported as still frames; this is sufficient only for very small, low-quality printing. You should also be well-versed in handling other aspects, such as color, interlacing, and picture and pixel aspect ratios when it comes to converting video to different formats.

Exporting a Movie Using a Preset

You can extract the whole sequence or just a selected segment from the timeline and save it as a file. You can even transform a clip into a full-length film if you choose. This approach is useful for creating a new version that uses a different compression type or format, or for constructing a movie from a single section of a clip.

To export a movie using a preset:

    1. **Do any of the following options:**

To export the sequence that has been modified in the timeline, pick either the Timeline view of the Monitor window or the Timeline window alone. To export a clip, you must first open a video clip in the Clip view of the Monitor window.

2. Select one of the following options to specify the footage that you want to export:

The first step is to position the work area bar in the timeline such that it is over the range of the timeline that you wish to export. You need to establish the in and out points of a clip before you can specify the frames you want to export.

3. From the drop-down option that appears when you click the Export icon on the taskbar, choose the format that best suits your movie:

    a. MPEG

    b. QuickTime

    c. Windows Media

At this point, the **Export Format dialog box** will appear. Which dialog box appears and what it says are both affected by the format you choose.

The left side of the dialog box lists the available presets; from this list, choose the one that best suits your output goal.

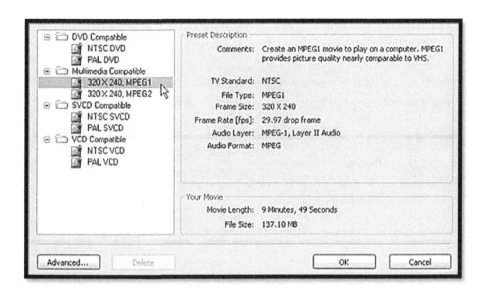

An overview of the settings linked to the selected preset is shown in the Preset Description portion of the dialog box. The part labeled "**Your Movie**" displays the expected size of the exported file.

    4.   To close the dialog box, choose **OK**.

A Save File dialog box appears.

    5.   Name the exported video file and choose a destination folder.

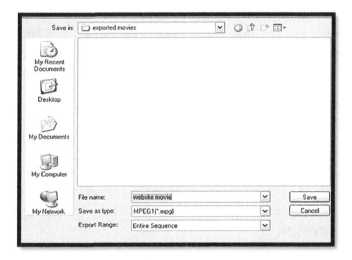

    6.   Select any of these options from the drop-down menu on the Export Range tab:

- When exporting a clip, you will be prompted to decide whether you want to export the full clip or only the frames that fall between the In point and Out point that you have defined.
- You'll be asked to choose whether you want to export the whole sequence or only the frames below the timeline's work area bar when you export a sequence.

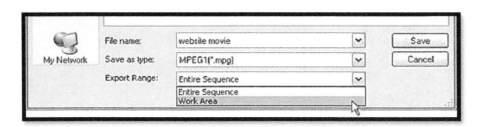

7. Pressing the **Save** button will cause the file to be rendered and exported.

After loading the file, Premiere Elements uses the preset to generate the final product. The file's size and application compatibility are both affected by the preset you choose.

TIPS

- While there are a variety of motivations for exporting a video file, the end goal is often to compress a large movie. However, DV movie files are still too large to be utilized on any medium other than DVDs, especially for CD-ROM or internet distribution, despite their comparatively tiny video size.
- Go to the menu bar, and then choose **File**, then **Export**, and finally **Movie** to export a movie file. However, you'll have to be more hands-on when choosing the export video quality if you want to utilize this method. Frame rate, audio quality, compression, and size are some of these factors.

Creating DVDs

Using a DVD burner and Premiere Elements, you can create DVDs that are compatible with the vast majority of DVD players. Before delving into the responsibilities, let's review the process.

Autoplay and menus

The DVD you make in Premiere Elements might have a dual purpose, depending on the option you select:
- When you insert the disc into the player, AutoPlay DVD will automatically create a copy of the disc that starts playing from the beginning. You can't use the navigation menus to

trigger scenes, but you can use the standard player controls like Play, Stop, Rewind, and Fast Forward.

- DVD with Menus is a tool that lets you create DVDs with additional features like a menu with buttons that trigger the scenes you choose. You may customize the DVD menu in Premiere Elements by selecting a template from the DVD Layout window. You may designate scenes, or chapters, in the timeline by placing DVD markers.

DVD menus

You can add a scene menu to your DVD by following these two easy procedures, which can be done in any order you like:

- **Add DVD Markers—.** It works the same way as DVD markers' timeline markers do. However, they find spots in the sequence that are used in the DVD player menus, instead of indicating crucial areas for editing. They mark the exact locations of the DVD's main menu, scenes (chapters), and the points at which it loops back to the main menu. The Timeline pane allows you to manually set DVD markers. From the main menu bar or the DVD Layout window, you can now give Premiere Elements the option to automatically set scene markers.
- **Modify a DVD Template.** Using Premiere Elements' built-in DVD Layout window, you can choose from a choice of pre-made menu layouts that cover a wide range of topics. Among these themes are several options for **entertainment, birthdays, and new baby**. The DVD menu buttons will be created automatically using the DVD scene markers, but you may still customize them to your liking. Before burning a DVD, you may try it out in the Preview window. If everything looks and works as it should, then this is a good sign.

DVD

Digital Video Disc is another name for Digital Versatile Disc, which is the acronym for DVD. The majority of DVDs have two sides and one layer. In other words, the data is stored on only one side of the disk or at a certain depth from the disk's surface. These DVDs can hold up to 4.7 GB of data, which is over two hours of high-quality video in a DVD-compatible format. A compact disc (CD) may hold data up to 700 megabytes (MB) or 650 MB (MB), depending on the disk. The general public often has this data in the form of a copy-protected film that they may have acquired via retail or rental means. Having a DVD burner and the right software allows you to record any kind of data into a recordable DVD. With Premiere Elements, you may burn your movies on DVDs in a format that is compatible with the vast majority of players.

DVD Markers

The functionality of DVD markers is similar to that of the timeline markers. There are similar menu commands for setting, clearing, and cueing them. Therefore, such approaches will not be covered here.

DVD markers, in contrast to timeline markers, are only visible in the Timeline window's time ruler and do not appear in the Monitor window's Timeline view's time ruler. DVD markers resemble timeline markers visually; however, they are presented at the bottom half of the Timeline window, beside the work area bar, instead of the top half, where they belong to the time ruler.

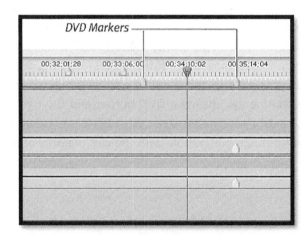

Unlike timeline markers, DVD markers in Premiere Elements' DVD Layout window provide links to buttons within a DVD menu you've constructed. **You can tell a DVD marker's function just by looking at its color:**

- **Green—.** Scene marker
- **Blue—.** Main menu marker
- **Red—.** Stop marker

Setting DVD markers

Premiere Elements has a button called **"DVD Marker"** that you can use to manually add DVD markers to the Timeline pane. The program can also automatically set scene markers at places in the sequence that match cuts or at intervals you specify. The option to automatically generate DVD scene markers is available in both the Timeline and DVD Layout windows. You may open these two windows separately if you want. **To add DVD markers manually:**

1. Go to the frame you want to mark and set the timeline's CTI to that frame.
2. In the Timeline window, click the **DVD Marker** button.

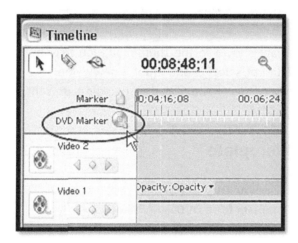

Clicking on the DVD Marker tool brings up its dialog box. In the dialog box, you can see a thumbnail of the video frame at the marker.

3. Naming the marker is essential.

Without delay, the DVD scene marker and chapter button's names are swapped.

4. Make your selection from the drop-down menu labeled **"Marker Type."**

The Scene Marker—. In addition to appearing as a green marker in the Timeline window, this function creates a Scene button in the DVD's scene menu.

The Main Menu Marker is —. The Timeline window will show this button as a blue marker, and it will also be generated on the DVD main menu.

Stop Marker—. At the time you specify, the DVD will go back to the main menu, as seen by the red marker in the Timeline window.

5. Ensure that the video frame at the marker appropriately represents the scene it is meant to if the **Thumbnail Offset** value needs adjusting.

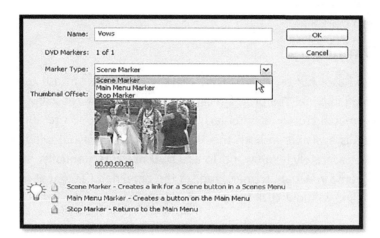

To have the frame you want shown in the thumbnail, you may either scrub the value that is presented below the picture or select it and input a new value. Press the OK button to dismiss the dialog window. Wherever the provided sort of marker is present in the timeline, it is at the CTI.

Choosing a DVD template

1. On the taskbar, locate the **DVD button** and click on it.
2. Select "**Apply a Template for a DVD with Menus.**"
3. In the Theme drop-down box, you may sort the available templates by category. Templates from the chosen category are shown in the main panel of the DVD Templates dialog box.
4. Use the scroll bar to look at all of the templates in that category. The left-hand thumbnail displays the template's main menu, while the right-hand thumbnail displays a Scenes menu.
5. You need to choose a menu template. There is a description of the template's button count on each page in the Template Details section of the dialog box.
6. Click **OK** to close the dialog box. The DVD Layout menu appears. On the Scenes Menu pages of the design, you can find the names and thumbnail images of the DVD scene markers placed throughout the sequence. "**Scene 1**," "**Scene 2**," and similar generic names are used when none are provided.

Exporting to Tape

By using the Export to Tape command in conjunction with an IEEE 1394 or other capture device, it is possible to transmit video to an attached camera or deck. It is possible to export any active clip in the Clip view, or more probably the sequence in the Timeline view and Timeline window. By using IEEE 1394 or an add-on device control, Premiere Elements can instantly activate your deck. At the beginning of the recording session, you have the option to choose the exact spot on the tape to start from if a timecode number is provided. But, to do this, your tape needs a timecode—at least at the beginning—on it. You may capture a timecode by recording a short movie (say, one or two minutes) while wearing the lens cap. Because of this, Premiere Elements will be able to automatically clip the tape using some timecode.

Exporting to tape

1. **Pick one option from the following:**
   o In either the Timeline or Monitor windows, choose the Timeline view to export a sequence.
   o Choose a clip to export from the Media window or open it in the Clip view of the Monitor window.
2. After you click the **Export** button in the taskbar, you'll get a pull-down menu. Choose **To Tape** from there.
3. If you want Premiere Elements to start recording automatically based on the device, go to the Activate Recording Device menu and choose one of the following options:

You can tell where you want the recording to start by looking for the phrase "Assemble at timecode"——on the tape. This option can only be used if the tape already has a timecode signal. This rule out the usage of blank tape. You can choose the number of frames to halt playback after clicking OK in the "Delay movie start by" area. The time it takes for certain recording devices to process the record command and for the video to be played back on a computer might vary. The "preroll" option controls the number of frames that will be rewound by the camera or deck before the start time, which may be either the timecode you chose for the "Assemble at timecode" option or the current position of the tape. This is done to ensure that the tape is going at the correct pace when recording begins.

4. In the Export to Tape dialog box's Options section, you can enter any of the following:

The message "**Abort after x dropped frames**"— gives you the option to specify the minimum number of failed frames before Premiere Elements stops recording. Even one dropped frame is unacceptable for the majority of users.

5. Press **Record**.

If the recording device is to be operated manually, be sure to switch it to record mode. If you want Premiere Elements to start recording right now, click the "**Activate Recording Device**" button. You can see how far along the export is in the Export to Tape dialog box's Export Status section.

Movie Files and Export Presets

Among the many possible uses for exporting a video file include creating a version that may be used in another application, sent over the internet, or played on a CD-ROM. With each distribution channel comes a plethora of media architectures, or format classifications. Various choices for determining the fundamental aspects of the movie, like frame size, frame rate, audio quality, etc., are available in every architecture. The options also dictate the codec or compression technique used for the file. One thing that the codec affects is the file's ultimate size and whether or not it is compatible with software. The good news is that Premiere Elements simplifies things by doing away with the requirement for you to understand and define a plethora of parameters. **Exporting a video file is one example of such a job. Premiere Elements is pre-set with the following:**

- Many sets of compression standards were developed by the Moving Picture Experts Group (MPEG, pronounced "em-peg"). Some of the formats that carry the moniker of the organization are MPEG-1 and MPEG-2. (The most popular audio format, MPEG-layer 3, is its formal name.)
- QuickTime—. There is a vast array of codecs developed for different uses included in the multimedia architecture of Apple systems.
- Windows Media is the protocol that Microsoft suggests for applications that do not need a high data rate, such as those that download music and video from the web.

Exporting a Movie Using a Preset

To make a new file, you can utilize the timeline sequence in its whole or part. You can also use a clip to make a movie. You can use this approach to create a full-length movie from a single clip or a modified version that uses a different format or compression. **To export a movie using a preset:**
   1. **Please choose an option from the following:**
To save the modified sequence from the timeline, choose the Timeline view in either the Monitor window or the Timeline window. You can export a video clip by opening it in the Clip view of the Monitor window.
   2. To export just the videos you've chosen, choose one of these options:
Set the work area bar over the timeline range that you wish to export in. You can choose which frames to export by adjusting the clip's In and Out points.
   3. Select the output format for your video by going to the Export option in the taskbar:
      o MPEG
      o QuickTime

o   Windows Media

An export format dialog box opens. This dialogue box will have a different name and different contents depending on the format you choose. On the left side of the dialog box, you should see the presets for your output objective. Pick one of them.

4. To close the dialogue window, click **OK**.
5. Choose an export destination and give the movie file a name.
6. In the Export Range drop-down menu, choose an option from the following:

You have the option to export the whole clip or only the frames between the in and out points when you export a clip. When exporting a sequence in the Timeline window, you can choose the full sequence or individual frames in the work area bar.

7. Press the **Save** button to export the file after rendering. This is how the file is rendered in Premiere Elements using the preset. The size of the file and its compatibility with programs are both affected by the settings you choose.

Exporting Single Still Images

It is possible to extract the most current frame from a video sequence or source clip and export it as a still image. **To export one frame:**

1. **Please choose an option from the following:**

To export a specific frame from a sequence, bring the Timeline view in the Monitor window to the desired frame. Select the desired frame to export by opening the Clip view in the Monitor window.

2. From the Monitor window, choose the **Export Frame button**.
3. Select **Settings**.
4. Select a **still-image format** using the **File Type drop-down** menu.
5. Pick one from the following:

To have the exported still photo opened instantly, use the "**Open When Done**" option. To configure the options for **CompuServe GIF** pictures, click on **Compile Options.**

6. To access the video settings, go to the Export Frame Options dialog box and choose **Video** on the left side.

After selecting Keyframe and Rendering to deinterlace the exported frame, choose **Deinterlace Video Footage** from the left side of the Export Frame Options dialog box. When taking still photographs from a movie with moving objects, you may sometimes see the combing effect; this option allows you to omit one field from the interlaced picture.

7. To close the Export Frame Options dialog box, press **OK** and return to the Export Frame dialog box.
8. Give the still picture a name and a location, then click Save. The format and location you choose are used to export the frame as a still-frame file.

Exporting Audio-Only Files

The process of exporting audio is the same as that of exporting a video and audio movie, with the exception that you can only utilize file types that solely include audio.

To export a file of audio:

1. **Please choose an option from the following:**

Selecting the sequence's tab in either the Timeline or Monitor windows will allow you to export audio from the timeline. To extract the audio from a clip, open it in the source view.

2. Select the movie you want to export by doing one of the following:

Position the work area bar over the timeline range that you want to export. By adjusting the clips In and Out points, you may choose which frames to export.

3. Pick **File > Audio Export.** A dialogue box to choose an audio format to export opens. At the very bottom of the dialog box, you can get a rundown of all the available export choices.

4. To change the current export settings, click the **Settings** button. After clicking Export Audio Settings, the General panel will appear in the dialog box.

5. The Export Audio Settings dialog box has many panels where you may change the export settings. To do this, choose a category from the left side of the box:

General— The general options include choosing the timeline range to export, the type of the audio file, and the inclusion or exclusion of a project link.

Audio— To provide settings that impact the sound, such as the rate of sampling and bit depth.

6. Click **OK** to dismiss the **Export Audio Settings** window.

7. Click **Save** once you've given your file a name and chosen a location. A progress bar displays the amount of time required to process the video.

CHAPTER 13

SHARING AND PUBLISHING YOUR VIDEOS

Share a movie on a mobile device

Downloading movies allows you to view them on mobile phones, some personal digital assistants, and portable media players such as video iPods and PlayStation Portable (PSP) devices. Premiere Elements has options that will activate some of these devices at the touch of a button. Altering the settings to match the aesthetic of a certain device is also an option.

Note:

One way to create video podcasts or vodcasts is to export them using an iPod or PSP setup.

- **Consult Device User Guide**: If you want to know what kinds of video files your mobile device can play, the first place to go is in the user manual or specifications. The compatibility of shared video files with different devices may be better assured with this data.

- **Navigate to the "Publish and Share"** option in Adobe Premiere Elements to access the Publish and Share panel. It will open the Publish and Share panel when you click on it.

- **Choose Mobile Phones And Players**: To choose mobile phones and players, go to the **"Publish and Share"** section of the page and look for the **"Mobile Phones and Players"** option. Selecting this option will provide a selection of themes optimized for various mobile devices.

- **Choose Your Player**: Pick your preferred player or device from the drop-down menu located at the screen's top. Use this setting to guarantee that your shared video is properly formatted for the device you're using.

- **Choose a Preset**: After the device has been selected, you may access its available settings by navigating to the Preset menu. To get the most out of your game, use the presets to choose the ideal file format, frame rate, and other parameters. Just below the name of the selected option, you'll see some details about it.

- **Name Your File and Choose a Location**: Choose a suitable name for your video clip and save it to a suitable location. Press the "Browse" button to choose a location on your computer to save the copied file.

- **Click on the "Advanced"** option for more detailed editing. You can make small changes to other settings here to suit your tastes or the needs of your project.

- **Save Changes as a New Preset:** If you make changes to an existing preset and then wish to utilize those same settings again, you may create a new preset from the existing one. For comparable projects or devices in the future, it will be straightforward to access these customized settings.

Note: You may have to fiddle with the 3GP settings to transmit a video that will play on a certain 3GP phone. To discover what your phone requires, read the handbook that comes with it. In addition, Premiere Elements's exported 3GP file format isn't compatible with all mobile devices.

- **Save it:** Premiere Elements converts your video into a file format that is compatible with your device.

About mobile formats

Thanks to device-specific settings in Adobe Premiere Elements, sharing your film on certain mobile devices is a breeze. These settings will provide the clearest possible playing. However, if your project requires more precise parameters, you may adjust them using the "Advanced" option. **Before making the switch from Premiere Elements to a mobile device, consider the following:**

1. **Using settings**:

Premiere Elements' settings are tailor-made for certain mobile devices, including Apple's iPods, iPads, and iPhones. These presets are optimized for use with certain devices, such as the iPod and iPhone, and you may choose between High Quality and Medium Quality settings.

2. **Understanding Preset Settings**:

Every preset has its own unique set of parameters, including file type, frame rate, file size, length, music frequency, and frame rate. These characteristics, shown under the preset name, might assist you in selecting the most suitable preset.

3. **Available Formats for Mobile Sharing**:

Apple iPod, iPad, and iPhone: Settings optimized for use with Apple's portable media players (iPod, iPad, and iPhone) are available. Customized settings for these devices allow you to choose between High Quality and Medium Quality.

Audio Podcast: With the "Audio Podcast" option, you may create an MPEG-4 Movie audio file, which is compatible with many portable media players, smartphones, and iPods. There are several alternatives available to you, including audio podcasts in high quality, medium quality, mono, and MP3 audio podcasts in medium quality.

4. **H.264 Compression Standard**:

Files produced with Premiere Elements for mobile devices are compressed using the H.264 standard. This compression technology guarantees minimal file sizes without sacrificing video quality, making it ideal for mobile viewing.

5. **Advanced Customization**:

If the pre-set choices aren't quite right, you can always click the "Advanced" button to fine-tune the export parameters to your precise specifications. You may transmit your video in a format that works on multiple mobile devices using Premiere Elements. For optimal playback on all devices and platforms, use these presets or tweak the parameters in the Advanced menu.

Share Your Photos and Videos

Making videos using Adobe Premiere Elements is so entertaining that you can overlook the most crucial step: sharing your finished products with others. Making entertaining and informative movies out of raw video footage is a common hobby. There is a plethora of options for sharing your completed films with the world. Here you can find the necessary steps to share your film work online. Here you can find guidance on navigating the specific challenges of uploading movies to the web, selecting appropriate player software, and exporting your finished projects in Web-friendly formats straight from Adobe Premiere Elements. Additionally, I teach you how to upload your videos to YouTube.

Archiving Movies on Photoshop.com

For some reason, the first time I ever let a record sit in full sunlight close to a window will stay with me forever. The data remained inaccessible and corrupted when I returned a few hours later. Taken aback! I wish I had a spare one! Hard drives, rather than record LPs, hold the majority of material these days. Data loss is still a real possibility in the digital era, even though computers won't wilt in direct sunlight. If your hard drive suddenly stops working, you can lose all of your media files, including music, pictures, and videos. However, this Adobe service allows Photoshop.com users to back up their images and videos online. **Follow these steps:**

1. Navigate to the Task pane and choose the Share option to distribute your changes.
2. When prompted with a variety of internet-sharing options, choose Photoshop.com.
3. After you've given your video a name, click "Next."
4. Select the number of viewers you would want to share the film with:
- **Everyone**: Anyone with an Internet connection can see your film.
- **People I Invite**: You can quickly send out request emails using the "People I Invite" feature, which allows you to choose who may see the video.
- **Private**: Only you with a Photoshop.com account will be able to see the video.
5. Just put a message into the **Email Message field** and check the boxes next to the individuals you want to invite to view the video.

To send out movie invites, Premiere Elements maintains a list of friends. To add friends, go to the contacts list and look for the "**Address Book**" icon in the upper right corner. Something human-like appears. Click **Add Contact** and input the name and email address of the person you want to add to your Address Book. To exit the Address Book, choose "**Done**."

6. Start sharing your video by clicking the **share** button.

The movie has to be compressed in the Photoshop.com video file first, so sharing it can take some time. There will be a link to your finished video on the website after the file is done.

Uploading Your Movies to YouTube

Internet connectivity and digital video are now as inseparable as Kirk and Spock. However, it was more reminiscent of the early days of digital television and the internet, when it was more like Spock and Dr. McCoy. Difficult and intricate, it was. If you wanted to upload photos to the web, you had to know how to create and administer websites as well as the means to pay for dedicated server space. Then, in 2005, YouTube emerged and revolutionized internet video viewing forever. **Some major changes occurred because of YouTube:**

- **Free Web server space**: Upload and view videos on YouTube without paying a dime.
- **Simple upload interface:** YouTube's uploading procedure is so straightforward that even someone without Internet experience can use it. You may easily transfer any video clip from your computer using the choices on the share page.
- **Flash video conversion:** Upload videos to YouTube in almost every popular video format. In an instant, YouTube will convert your videos to the Adobe Flash format. Nearly every new computer has the free Adobe Flash Player browser extension preinstalled.

Better still, you can upload your finished films to YouTube without any additional software at all thanks to Adobe Premiere Elements. Videos must be under 100 MB in size and no longer than 10 minutes to be posted. Aside from that, you need to adhere to YouTube's guidelines for appropriate content.

NOTE: YouTube is a treasure trove of knowledge, but be aware that some videos may include explicit material that is prohibited or otherwise objectionable in some regions. Various nations have blocked YouTube at various points in time, and some may even restrict access to certain kinds of videos. Similarly, some corporate networks do not allow YouTube videos. Never assume that your ideal YouTube audience will be able to see your videos.

Creating a YouTube account

You can upload videos to YouTube for free, but you'll need an account. Premiere Elements allows you to create an account during the upload process, or you may do it later on at any moment on the YouTube website:

1. Click the **"Sign Up"** link in the top right area of www.youtube.com.

A page that allows you to create an account appears.

2. Along with a password, provide a functional email address.

A minimum of eight characters long password with a mix of uppercase and lowercase letters, numbers, and symbols is required. To ensure a smooth account setup process, YouTube will send a confirmation email to the email address you provided. Please ensure that this address is accurate.

3. Create a distinct name for your account.

Use the **"Check Availability"** link to see whether your desired username is available.

4. Check out the Terms of Use and Privacy Policy files and enter any other information that is asked for.

The video-sharing website YouTube is curious about your gender and the country of your birth. The Privacy Policy and Terms of Service are available online for your review.

5. Press "**Create Account**."
6. Tap the "**Confirm your email address**" link that appears in the permission email from YouTube. You can access your email account by clicking here.

If you do not get the confirmation email, you should verify that it was not accidentally sent to the trash by checking the anti-spam settings of your email program or account.

Uploading the movie

Nearly any video clip on your computer can be uploaded to YouTube by visiting **www.youtube.com**, logging into your account, and searching for the "**Upload**" option on the YouTube page. Premiere Elements makes it easy to upload videos to YouTube, so there's no need to go through all that hassle. Be sure your PC has internet access if you want to see your edited film online after making adjustments in Premiere Elements. What follows is an order of business:

1. When a selection of sharing options appears, pick **Online** after clicking the **Share** tab.
2. Choose "**YouTube**" from the option to share online.

View your movie's duration and file size on the Share tab. Videos uploaded to YouTube using Premiere Elements were restricted to 100 MB in size and 10 minutes in duration. Your video has to be either edited further to make it shorter (less than ten minutes) or divided into sections (more than ten minutes) before it can be shared.

3. Use the **Presets** menu to choose a setting.

Upload your 4:3 movies to YouTube in the Flash Video format. If your movie is in a 16:9 aspect ratio, choose Flash Video for YouTube (Widescreen).

4. When prompted, enter your **YouTube credentials** after selecting "**Next**."

Select the box next to "**Remember Me**" to make logging in a breeze.

5. After that, you'll need to provide some facts about your film and press "**Next**" once more.

What viewers will see when they watch your YouTube video is this? Additionally, it facilitates YouTube's ability to discover your video.

6. Decide on who can see your film.

If you choose yes, your YouTube video will be accessible to everybody. Even if you choose "**No**," you may still invite some friends to view your video—all they need is a YouTube account, and you'll have to grant them access under your account settings. The "**Account**" page is where you can access your YouTube settings.

7. Click on the **Share** button.

Premiere Elements will convert your video to Flash before uploading it to YouTube. Depending on its length and complexity, the time required to make and upload your video will vary. A screen with a link to your video on YouTube will appear when the movie has finished uploading. To let other people see your video, send them an email with the URL. If your film isn't yet ready to view on YouTube, that's okay. The YouTube server must process the video first before it can play. By and large, this is a quick process.

Creating Web-Friendly Video Files

You may easily share your videos with everyone online thanks to YouTube since it's free. You don't have to limit yourself to YouTube, however. Video projects created with Premiere Elements may be saved in the most popular web-friendly formats. Among these kinds are Adobe Flash, Apple QuickTime, and Windows Media Video from Microsoft. You should be mindful of several technical concerns while uploading movies to the internet. Many decades ago, the Internet's creators had a noble goal: to make it easier for people all over the globe to exchange and access information. But the initial intention wasn't to share full-motion footage online. **There are primarily two reasons why videos, particularly live videos, do not function well with the current state of the Internet:**

- **Bandwidth**: What precisely is "**high speed**" when it comes to the Internet? High-speed broadband services have been more popular in recent years, but how fast is it? It may still take some time for large video files to download, and some of your viewers may not have the patience to wait for the downloads to complete. If other users on the Internet begin to enjoy your movies, large movie files may also consume your Web server's monthly data allotment rapidly.
- **Packet delivery**: Data is sent across the Internet in smaller groupings known as packets rather than in sluggish streams under the packet delivery method. Thus, data transmission via the Internet is secure yet slow.

NOTE

Bits are used to separate data before sending it over the Internet. There are several paths that these packets take to reach their destination. They are then reassembled in the correct sequence to form an online shareable file, such as a web page, email, or document. Contrast packet delivery with single-wave data transmission methods like radio or television broadcasts. Because neither the sender nor the receiver has to be online constantly, sending and receiving packets is completely secure. Still confused? Imagine you are across the room from the person you want to offer your phone number to. If you attempt to shout across the room (a broadcast), you may miss one or two numbers due to the background noise from the audience. To be on the safe side, jot down your number and utilize the message to communicate across the room. Printing out a number guarantees that the recipient has the correct number, although it takes more time.

Choosing Player Software

Make sure that the individuals you want to see your film can open the file format before you upload it to the internet for distribution. When using Premiere Elements, you have the option to use Flash, QuickTime, or Windows Media. To begin, uninstall Adobe Flash. Flash is used by video-sharing websites like YouTube, but it is not something you should employ to display videos on your site. The only ones that have been left out are Apple QuickTime and Microsoft Windows Media. Put simply, it's Microsoft going up against Apple. Tell me which one is superior. Although I've done a lot of work with Windows Media Video and QuickTime, I can state that neither is technologically superior. The files are both tiny and of decent quality. First and foremost, you must consider the program your customer is using.

You may download Apple's QuickTime player for Windows for free, and QuickTime is preinstalled on every Macintosh computer. Similarly, Windows Media Player is pre-installed on every new Windows PC. Flip4Mac is a free QuickTime plugin that allows Mac users to view Windows Media Video; it may be found on the Microsoft website. Direct support for Macs by Windows Media Player is not available from Microsoft. Would you want Windows Media or QuickTime? Have faith in your intuition. Choose the style that appeals to you the most. If site visitors are unhappy with the design you've chosen, you'll know exactly what they want. I don't see the value in bringing up capacity and frames in such a convoluted manner. You have to drastically reduce the frame size, compress the video, and sacrifice some quality when you produce video for the web.

On the Internet, you may distribute videos in two ways:

- **Download**: One option is to download the whole movie file before playing it. These days, you may start playing the movie even before it finishes downloading. To begin playing without interruption, the application determines when it has received sufficient footage from the movie. The process is similar to that of streaming video and goes by the names progressive playing and progressive download.

- **Stream**: With "stream," the user may listen to the soundtrack while the movie downloads to their computer. To keep playing without pausing, some of the video is delayed, which implies that some data is temporarily stored in computer memory. The three most common media players for streaming video are RealMedia, Windows Media Streaming Video, and Apple QuickTime Streaming. In each of these cases, specialized server software is required to manage live media.

Whatever method you decide to use to distribute the video, the procedure of exporting it from Adobe Premiere Elements remains the same. You may transmit the movie by saving it to your hard disk.

TIP: You may want to consider making a lower-quality video for those who experience anxiety or have sluggish dial-up connections. You should perhaps build a better movie for those who have fast internet. Make sure to consider making variants that can be played by more than one person. Versions of Windows Media and Apple QuickTime are acceptable here. It's no secret that some individuals are quite particular about the software developers they work with.

Saving an Apple QuickTime movie

A lot of people use Apple QuickTime to distribute movies online since there's a decent balance between file size and quality. Sending a QuickTime file requires QuickTime Player 6 or later to be installed on your computer. Download QuickTime from Apple's website at www.apple.com. Once QuickTime is installed, exporting a movie is a breeze. **Once you have finished editing your video, be sure to:**

1. Select **Personal Computer** from the drop-down menu under the **Share tab** to begin sharing.
2. Select **QuickTime** from the PC sharing options menu located at the top of the page.
3. Click on the **Presets** menu and choose a **setting**.

At the very bottom of the Share tab, you'll see a notice about the option you just selected. In the options, you may find several combinations of frame rate, audio frequency, and frame size to accommodate different bandwidth requirements. On a LAN, everything works well. The audio frequency is 44 kHz, and the frame rate is either 29.97 fps (PAL) or 25 fps (NTSC), all of which are comparable to CD quality. The screen size is 640 × 480. Selecting the 128K Dual ISDN option reduces the image resolution to 320 × 240, slows the frame rate to 15 fps, and lowers the sound quality to 16 kHz. If you're still having trouble after trying those two choices, you may always go into the export preferences by clicking the "Advanced" button. More complex QuickTime preferences will be covered in the next section.

4. You can name your video in the **File Name field**.
5. To choose a location to save the video, just click the **Browse** button.
6. **Save** it.

When you click **Save**, Premiere Elements begins to produce and save the movie. You may monitor the export's progress with the help of a rendering progress meter. You can also see how much time is remaining on the progress indicator. The file-saving process could be lengthy if the project is lengthy.

Choosing advanced QuickTime settings

Utilizing a preset is a better option if you wish to choose the export parameters for a QuickTime movie rather than manually customizing them. Click the Advanced button on the Share tab while you are exporting a QuickTime video to make adjustments to the parameters. By clicking the tabs in the **Export Settings box**, you may access more sophisticated settings for the video and audio for the export. After you have finished making changes to the parameters in the Export parameters box, click the **OK** button and continue exporting your video in the same manner as we discussed before.

Adjusting QuickTime video settings

When you enter the dialog box for exporting settings, the advanced video settings should be the first item that you see. Considering that QuickTime movies are videos, this makes perfect sense. Discovering your way around the QuickTime video settings is not the most difficult thing to do. **To review the following options, go to the Video tab under the Export options box and look at them:**

- **Codec**: This is the procedure that is used to reduce the size of the video file by compressing and decompressing it. In most cases, the H.264 codec is the most suitable option from the Codec selection when it comes to usage online. Individuals may have difficulty seeing your QuickTime videos if they play jerkily. Consider using one of the Sorenson codecs as an alternative.

- **Quality**: This value controls how the video picture is reduced in size. There is no need to be surprised by the fact that files of higher quality are larger.

- **Frame Width/Height**: The width and height of the frame are the boxes that allow you to modify the size of the video picture. To prevent the video picture from being distorted, it is recommended that the aspect ratio be maintained at 4:3. In QuickTime Player, widescreen movies with a 16:9 aspect ratio will be letterboxed.

- **Frame Rate**: A frame rate of 25 or 29.97 frames per second (fps) is considered to be the standard for video captured at broadcast quality. With a frame rate of 12 or 15 frames per second, you may conserve both space and data. If you want to make sure that the gaming is running smoothly, choose a frame rate that is either half or a third of the original frame rate.

- **Field Order**: When it comes to watching movies online, you often choose None (Progressive) as your field order. You have the option of selecting either Upper or Lower if, on the other hand, the video you are creating has issues with combing or other forms of interlacing.

- **Pixel Aspect Ratio:** Square Pixels are the most common option in this part of the process; but, if the video picture you are working with seems to be compressed or stretched, you may need to choose one of the rectangle pixel combinations. Select the alternative that is compatible with the format of the video that you are using in your task.

- **Set Bitrate:** Changing the video speed may be accomplished by moving the Bitrate tool and adding a tick to the box that is located next to the one that says Set speed. A greater bitrate implies a higher quality of video, but it also indicates that the files will be larger.

- **Set Key Frame Distance**: A more effective method of compressing video is to use keyframes. In situations when there is a longer period between keyframes, it is not uncommon for the file size and clarity to decrease. You may alter the amount of time that passes between compression keyframes by checking the box that reads "**Set Key Frame Distance.**"

If you choose this option, the compression will function considerably more effectively; but some individuals may have difficulty playing the files, particularly those who are using earlier versions of QuickTime. **NOTE:** It is important to note that compression keyframes and effect keyframes are not whatsoever the same, even though they have the same name. A compression keyframe is just what it sounds like a picture of the whole movie. A keyframe may only occur once every one, five, or even 10 seconds when the video is compressed. The frames that are located in between these significant frames are the only ones that display the changes that have occurred in the video picture. Frames like this are referred to as delta frames.

Adjusting QuickTime audio settings

Using Apple QuickTime's recording settings is a simple process. It is possible to use the AAC codec. You have the option of selecting a single or split output, an audio codec, and a frequency from the Codec menu inside the program. Although music at a frequency of 44 kHz sounds like it was recorded on a CD, it is important to bear in mind that high-quality audio may fast cause files to become larger. **TIP**: This is where you should begin reducing the size of your stored files if they are too large. You can get this information here. Some very little adjustments, like as switching from stereo to mono, may have a significant impact on the size of the file.

Exporting Windows Media

Adobe Premiere Elements has several file options, one of which is Windows Media, which is compatible with the web. Using this export option, you may create a **Windows video Video (WMV)** file, which is an excellent format for exporting video from the internet. Video in the WMV format may be downloaded via progressive download, which is sometimes referred to as recommended download. This indicates that the video begins to play as soon as sufficient data has been received, ensuring that it plays continuously from the beginning to the finish of the film. There is a free Windows Media Player application included with every single Windows computer. A free application known as Flip4Mac is available on the websites of both Apple and Microsoft for users of Macintosh computers. This tool enables users to watch WMV files that have not been encrypted. The production of videos using Windows Media is quite similar to the production of movies using QuickTime. **You may share a video created with Windows Media by following these steps:**
1. Click the **Share tab** when you're done making changes to your movie.
2. Pick the option to share a personal computer.

Even though you want to post it online in the end, you should not choose the "**Online**" option. When you choose the "**Online**" option, you will only be able to view Flash video kinds.
3. Choose **Windows Media** from the menu at the top of the PC share options.

4. From the **Presets** menu, pick a **setting**.

As soon as you choose an option, a notification about that setting will appear at the bottom of the Share tab. To accommodate a wide variety of bandwidth requirements, the settings allow for the selection of a variety of combinations of frame size, frame rate, and audio frequency. If you are dealing with high-definition video, the HD 1080i and 720p configurations will provide you with the most favorable outcomes. Even though the files are often considerably too large to be used online, the playing quality of these settings is very nearly equivalent to that of broadcast quality. The most web-friendly environment is a local area network, sometimes known as a LAN. With a frame size of 640 × 480, a frame rate of 30 frames per second (NTSC) or 25 frames per second (PAL), and an audio frequency of 44 kilohertz, it is comparable to the quality of a CD. A distinction may be made between this and the DialUp 56K Modem setting, which is the one with the lowest grade. With a frame size of 176 × 144, a frame rate of 10 frames per second, and a sound frequency of 16 kHz, this particular configuration is used. The LAN option, as you would anticipate, results in a much improved playing quality; nevertheless, the files are significantly larger as a consequence. If you are unable to locate a configuration that is suitable for your needs, you may build your export settings by clicking the "**Advanced**" option. It is important to note that, similar to QuickTime, video files that employ settings that have a higher frame rate, larger frame sizes, or better audio quality tend to be larger. Make adjustments to the parameters for exporting Windows Media files by selecting the "**Advanced**" option. In the next section, I will discuss the more sophisticated settings.

5. In the **File Name field**, give your movie a name.

If you want to distribute your video in more than one size so that it may be seen by a broad variety of people online, you need to make sure that the filename corresponds to the setting that was used for this version. The Cable Modem/DSL option may be used in one version of a movie that was filmed during a jazz festival. In this case, you may call the file JazzFestDSL. It is possible that JazzFest56K would be the name of a second version that takes advantage of the 56K Modem option.

6. Just click **Browse** and pick a place to save the movie.

7. **Save** it.

When you click the **Save** button, Premiere Elements will begin the process of creating and saving the movie. A rendering progress bar will appear to provide you with information on the status of the export. When you look at the progress indicator, you may also get a sense of how much time is remaining. Should this be a lengthy project, the process of saving the file can take some time.

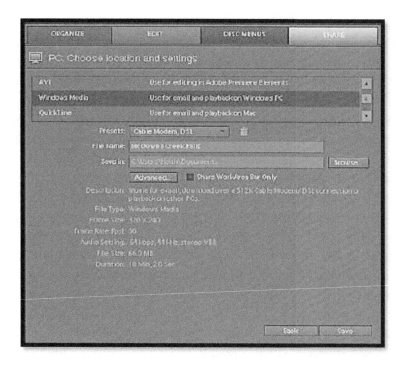

Customizing Windows Media settings

The Windows Media export settings ought to be able to fulfill the majority of your requirements. You may make adjustments to the settings by selecting the Advanced option on the Windows Media sharing screen. The Export Settings box has tabs for Video settings, Audio settings, and Audiences. These tabs are located inside the box. **In these settings, you should try to avoid injuring your hands:**

- **Video Codec**: On the Video tab, you will find a selection of Windows Media codecs from which to choose. Additionally, your video will be compatible with previous versions of Windows Media Player because you have the option to use older versions of the Windows Media codec, such as 7 or 8. If an individual attempts to view a video generated by Windows Media Video 9 on Windows Media Player 7 or 8, the movie may not function properly or might not play at all. There is not much of a purpose to utilize an earlier version of Windows Media Player after the release of Windows Media Player 9 in the year 2003.

- **Allow Interlaced Processing**: In the Video options, you also have the option to choose interlaced processing. If the videos you transmit have difficulties with interlacing, such as cutting or other problems, choose this option.

- **Bitrate Settings**: From the list that is located next to Encoding Passes, choose two Encoding Passes to use for the Bitrate Settings. If you choose this option, the process of sending the movie will take longer, but it will also help the video shrink more effectively.

If you need to send the video out as soon as possible, choose Only One Encoding Pass. Selecting the Variable Unconstrained option is your best chance if you want to get higher quality and greater compression while using the Bitrate Mode.

- **Frame Width/Height**: These boxes allow you to modify the size of the video picture that you are working with. It is recommended that the aspect ratio be maintained at 4:3 to prevent the video picture from being distorted. In Windows Media Player, videos with a 16:9 aspect ratio will be shown with a letterbox.
- **Frame Rate**: A frame rate of 25 or 30 frames per second (fps) is considered to be the standard for video that is of broadcast quality. With a frame rate of 12 or 15 frames per second, you may conserve both space and data. If you want to make sure that the gaming is running smoothly, choose a frame rate that is either half or a third of the original frame rate.
- **Pixel Aspect Ratio:** Square Pixels are the excellent selection for this situation most of the time; but, if the video picture you are working with seems to be compressed or stretched, you may need to choose one of the rectangular pixel alternatives instead. Select the alternative that is compatible with the format of the video that you are using in your task.
- **Keyframe Interval**: The usage of keyframes for compression results in a decreased size of the video. In situations when there is a longer period between keyframes, it is not uncommon for the file size and clarity to decrease. Changes may be made to the Keyframe Interval to alter the amount of time that passes between compression keyframes.
- **Video Bitrate**: This slider gives you the ability to modify the average level of the video bitrate. It is surprising to learn that greater bitrates result in files that are both larger and of higher quality.
- **Audio settings**: Just as with video, you can choose an audio codec and bitrate level on the Audio page. Video options are also available.
- **Audiences:** When you export the movie, you will have the option to choose whether or not it will be compressed by selecting the Audiences tab.

NOTE: If you do not care about the size of the file in any manner, you should always choose Compressed. Where does it become irrelevant?

After you have finished reviewing and modifying the Windows Media export options, you can exit the Export options dialog box by clicking the **OK** button.

CHAPTER 14

ORGANIZING AND MANAGING YOUR MEDIA LIBRARY

Using the Organizer for Media Management

As you continue to edit more and more projects in Premiere, the quantity of video and other media clips that you have to deal with might rapidly become daunting. To get to the destination, all that is required is a few excursions, a few family get-togethers, and perhaps a few school assignments. While you are suffering media overload, you pick the Organize tab in Premiere and search through a large number of clips. However, you are unable to find the clip that you are searching for with any success. You must locate a solution for controlling your media files. If you are working with Premiere, choose the **Organize tab,** and then click the **Organizer button** located in the upper-right corner of the screen. The fact that the Organize button on the splash screen starts the Elements Organizer program contributes to the confusion that previously existed between the terms Organizer and Organize. Regardless of how you activate it, Organizer provides a presentation of your media clips that are somewhat distinct from Premiere's Organize tab, as well as functions that are somewhat distinct from those included inside it. You may also tell that they are rather different from one another if you look at them carefully and pay attention to the details. For example, you are unable to generate or make use of keyword tags inside the Organize tab of Premiere; but, you can do so using the Organizer. Additionally, you are only able to build albums using the Organizer component of Premiere. Make use of the Organizer tool to organize, categorize, and manage your ever-growing collection of media products. While you are editing videos, you may see your content by utilizing the Organize tab in Premiere.

Tour the Organizer

The Organizer displays all of the media assets that you import in a miniature format, including movies, photographs, and music. These assets are organized in rows and columns in a precise manner. Considering that the Organizer was initially developed as a tool for organizing images in Photoshop Elements, the screen looks like a lightbox used by photographers. This is a fitting comparison given that this book will refer to the primary screen of the Organizer as "the lightbox." Adobe refers to this collection of media files as your catalog within the program. There is a navigation bar located at the very top of the Organizer screen that gives you the choice to view and import your clips respectively. It is possible to import files from your camera or computer by selecting the File Get Photographs and Video option, for instance. Under the Find menu of the Organizer, you can see your clips in several different ways, such as by the kind of file or by the corresponding date. Is it necessary for you to locate the footage of the hummingbird that you captured seven months ago? There is no problem. There is a search box and a slider that allows you to change the size of your thumbnail photographs in the area that is located underneath the navigation bar. **A Tasks panel may also be found on the right side of the lightbox. This panel is comprised of four tabs, which are as follows:**

- **Organize:** The Organizer is where you will spend most of your time since it is primarily used for organizing your clips, which is one of its primary functions. You can give keywords to your clips, enable you to search for them at a later time, score your clips on a scale from 0 to 5, and arrange them into albums. Every one of these approaches helps you locate the material you want in a short amount of time while you are editing a project.

- **Fix:** The Fix tab is used to rectify still photographs. It offers capabilities like Auto Red Eye Repair, Auto Contrast, and Auto Color, which may be used to improve the contrast and color balance of a picture without altering the color of the image itself.

- **Create:** On the Create tab, you will be able to see the beginnings of the Organizer, which are still photographs. A significant number of the options are concerned with activities such as the production of greeting cards, calendars, and photo albums. As a videographer, the buttons that you will most likely click on are the Slide Show button, the Instant Movie button, and the DVD with Menus button. Whenever you click on the latter two, the Organizer will take you to Premiere. The Organizer, for example, launches Premiere and shows the InstantMovie window if you choose **InstantMovie** as the application program.

- **Share:** The Sharing tab provides users with the ability to produce DVDs and Blu-ray discs, as well as publish movies on the internet. Sharing options are also accessible. Neither of the options will take you anywhere other than Premiere.

Import Media to the Organizer

The Organizer will automatically show any content that you import into Premiere; nevertheless, it is beneficial to have the ability to import video, audio, and still photos directly into the Organizer itself. This is because the Organizer is the same tool that you use to categorize the media, which includes rating, tagging, and assigning it to certain albums. You can import content from a wide range of devices, such as PCs, camcorders, and cameras (both still and video). If you want to import video from a tape-based DV or HDV camera, you will need to use Premiere Elements and follow the processes that are detailed on the Navigation buttons. This is because the Organizer does not have a Device Control feature.

Import Media from a Camera

The following are the several methods that may be used to directly import content from a tapeless camcorder into the Organizer:

1. Bring your camera into connection with your PC. Several camcorders make use of a USB cable. Certain models, such as the most recent mini-camcorders from the Flip brand of cameras, are equipped with a USB port that is built right into the camera apparatus.
2. Select the **File** menu, and then select the option to "**Get Picture and Videos from Camera or Card Reader in the Organizer.**"
3. The Pick a Device option allows you to select the camcorder that you want to use. Both Windows and the Organizer will see your camcorder as a storage device that can be detached from its housing. A drive letter, such as E: or F, is also present in this instance.
4. You can choose certain clips by clicking the option labeled "**Advanced Dialog.**" If you want to import all of the content from your camcorder, you may skip this step. When you click the Advanced Dialog button, you will be presented with a list of all the files from which you may choose. Click the checkboxes that are located next to the clips that you want to import.
5. Press **Get Media.**

The footage from your camcorder is transferred to your computer via the Organizer. Both the Organize tab and the Organizer that are available in Premiere are where you may locate the imported content.

Import Media from PC Files and Folders

Pay attention to the following techniques to extract media from a folder or file on your computer:

1. Select **File > Get Photo and Videos > From Files and Folders** in the Organizer from the menu that appears. It is then that the window labeled Get Photographs and Videos Files and Folders displays. There is also the option to open this window by pressing Ctrl+Shift+G.
2. You will need to choose the files or folders that you want to import. Select a folder to import all of the material that is included inside it, or double-click the folder to select individual files to import using the import command. Apply the following basic selection strategies to choose several files:

To choose, click on the option. To choose files that are related, use the **Shift** key. To select or deselect multiple files, you can use the **Control** key. You can import several files simultaneously by clicking and dragging them into the text box.

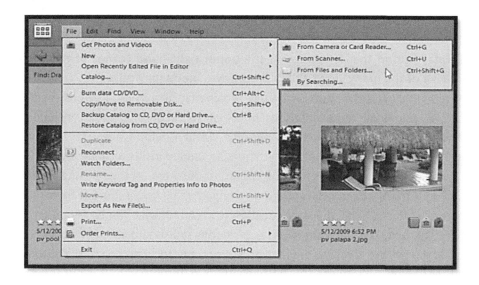

3. Press **Get Media.**

It is the organizer that is responsible for importing the clips into your library. The Organize tab of Premiere is another place where you may see the same clips. After you have imported your clips into the Organizer, they will be shown in the lightbox and can be accessed via the Organize tab in Premiere.

Change Views in the Organizer

If your project has just twenty media clips, it is possible that you will not need the aid of the Organizer. When you have a total of 200 clips, you will be able to begin to comprehend the matter. Additionally, if you have more than 2,000 clips that are spread out across several different projects, you will want the ability to organize your clips. **The organizer came to the rescue! Here is how things work out:**

1. Click the **Organize** icon that is located on the splash screen of Premiere to access the Organizer. As an alternative, you can access the Organizer straight from inside Premiere by clicking the Organize tab and then the Organizer button immediately thereafter.
2. If the **Show All button** is present, click on it.

Display of the Show All button is contingent upon the fact that you have previously filtered the lightbox view while working inside the same session. Because of this, if you were using a filtered view in the lightbox (for example, See Pictures), then switched to another window to complete a task, and then returned to the lightbox, the filter would continue to be active. When you are in this circumstance, click the Show All button to access all of your files. Despite this, the lightbox will always return to the Show All mode once the Organizer program is discontinued. Likely, you will not be aware of the Display All option since the Organizer displays all of your files by default.

3. Take advantage of the **Display menu** to arrange and show your clips in a variety of different ways.

Click the Display button that is located in the upper right-hand corner of the Organizer. The following is a list of the many views that a drop-down menu may offer:

- The default view is the Thumbnail View, which may be accessed by pressing Ctrl+Alt+1. It displays thumbnail representations of all of your content, which includes audio and video clips, as well as digital photographs. Creating albums and tagging films is made much simpler by the fact that everything is contained inside a single archive.

- When you import your clips into the Organizer, they are arranged using the Import Batch function (Ctrl+Alt+2), which is based on the dates that you imported them.

- There is a shortcut called Folder Location (Ctrl+Alt+3) that can be found on the left side of the lightbox. This shortcut exposes a sidebar that is similar to Windows Explorer and details the folders that are present on your computer. The process of opening a folder and clicking on a file to see it is probably quite natural to you. It is not the case that The Organizer functions in such a manner; in fact, it is the complete reverse. If you are using this mode, the folder that the file is located in will be shown in the sidebar on the left when you click on a file in the lightbox.

- You may think of this view as a tool that will provide you with information on the placement of the video clips on your computer. It is consistent with the "all-in-one-big-pool" concept that the Elements Organizer proposes. If you want to move a clip from the lightbox to another folder, you may do so by dragging it. According to what was previously said, you should not use Windows to transfer material that has been imported. If you happen to do so, the file will no longer be visible to the Organizer. Utilizing this view is another option for transferring clips across different directories.

- Date View, which can be accessed by pressing **Ctrl+Alt+D,** displays a calendar that highlights the dates that you imported files. By altering the display, the calendar may be seen in the order of the year, the month, or the day. If you click on a date that is highlighted, you will be able to see the imported content for that specific day.

- The function F11 allows for full-screen viewing, editing, and organizing. In this mode, most of the organizer features are concealed, providing you with an excellent view of your material in its entirety. Under collapsible menus on the left side of the screen, you will find a modest collection of tools that facilitate the modification of your content (such as Smart Fix and Auto Color, for example) and the organization of your material (such as Add to Album and Add Keyword). To return to the default display, use the Esc key.

- Comparing similar photographs (F12). The sole distinction between this full-screen view and the one mentioned before is that the Organizer displays two thumbnails of photos or videos next to one another. This is the entire variation between the two. You have the option of selecting the pictures you want to compare in advance by using the Ctrl-click shortcut, or you may make changes to the images after you are presented with them. Click on the image, and then use the arrow buttons that appear at the bottom of the screen to navigate around the media collection you have created from scratch.

4. Within the lightbox of the Organizer, you can select whether to show or hide certain types of material, exactly as you may do in the Organize tab of Premiere.

For instance, click View Media Types and uncheck Photographs, Projects, and PDF to see just video and audio files. Ensure that only Video and Audio are chosen.

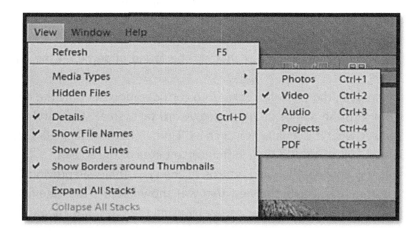

5. It is possible to adjust the size of your thumbnail photographs by clicking and dragging the slider to the top center of the window. You may adjust the slider to the right to display thumbnails that are larger but less in number. By moving the slider to the left, you may see thumbnails that are smaller yet more numerous.

6. Tap the **Date menu** that is located next to the slider to arrange the thumbnails in chronological order. There are two options available to choose from inside the Date menu (Oldest First): Date (Newest First) and Date. According to Newest First, the most recent collection of films that you imported is the one that is highlighted. When viewing films from events that have a distinct chronology, such as a wedding or birthday celebration, it is useful to see the material in the order in which it was captured.

7. Next to the Date menu, choose the **Details checkbox** you want to go with. When you choose Details, more information is shown underneath each clip (assuming that the thumbnails you have selected are sufficiently big).

When you connect tags and albums to your clips, you will not be able to see the symbols that are associated with those tags and albums. Verify that the thumbnail slider is set to a size that will display the file names, and check to see whether the display of the filenames is enabled by choosing View Show Filenames. Whether the file names are not visible, check that the slider is set to the appropriate size. [It is crucial to know that while you are in the View menu, you can utilize the keyboard shortcut Ctrl+D to expose and hide file information by choosing View information.]

8.   Either the scroll wheel on your mouse or the scroll bar that is shown to the right of the lightbox may be used to browse between the clips that you have selected. Raise or lower the scroll bar to go across the page more quickly. Simply clicking the top and bottom arrows of the bar will allow you to move a row at a time.

You may change the amount of space that is available for your thumbnails by sliding the bar that separates the lightbox from the Task panel to the left or right. You will see that the horizontal bar that divides the Albums screen from the Keyword Tags panel is identical. If one of the panels is closed, you may open it by clicking the triangle icon that is attached to it.

9.   Take advantage of the search box that can be found underneath the navigation bar to search.

During the search process, the Organizer takes into consideration not only the names of the files being searched, but also the names of albums, keyword tags, smart tags, and dates. When it is searching, you can see what it is looking for, such as "Find: Items matching 10/12/2009."

10.   The blue Back arrow may be seen in the top-left area of the screen.

When the date filter is applied, the view returns to the view that was previously shown. When you hit the back button once again, the view that was shown before the date filtering is brought into view. You may go through your view history by using the Back and Forward arrows on your interface. Now that you have developed your abilities as a viewer, it is a fantastic idea to learn how to rate and filter clips, which are also referred to as filtering your collection.

Rank your Clips with Star Ratings

Imagine that you take your camcorder with you and spend the whole day filming buffalo by yourself. At home, you will import your footage, and then you will be able to start editing. However, when all you see is a thumbnail image of each clip, it may be difficult to differentiate between the buffalo video that is of high quality and the footage that is of low quality. Even though you may be anxious to get started on a project right away, you should leave yourself some time to sift through the clips and evaluate the good ones and those that are not good. In Premiere, star ratings provide a way that is both quick and easy to use for doing this. Within the Organizer lightbox (or picture or music), five little stars that have been ghosted out show under every clip individually. When you have finished watching each video, you may give it a rating by clicking on one of the stars. One way that has been tried and tested for deciding how to rate a clip is as follows: To differentiate between the two categories of clips, during the first pass, give clips that are valuable one star and clips that are not beneficial none. Proceed to choose one star from the Rating filter located in the upper-right-hand corner of the lightbox of the Organizer. This will allow you to hide the clips that you deemed to be of no benefit from your perspective. To boost the ratings of the useful clips to good and maybe even extraordinary as you continue to evaluate and compare material, you should give them two, three, or even more stars. (If you believe that you were either too generous or too thrifty, you have the option to go back and alter the rating.) In the process of editing your project, you can filter your clips based on their star rating, which is a time-saving method that, at first glance, may seem to be a laborious process. In this method, you will not be analyzing films that are of poor quality. For instance, if you only want to browse Buffalo movies that have gotten three stars or above, you may customize the rating filter by selecting the relevant star.

Apply Star Ratings

Rating your films is a very straightforward process. Simply choose one of the five stars that are shown next to the video. There is no difference in the procedure for assigning a star to a clip, regardless of whether you are in the Organize tab or the Organizer of Premiere. It is possible that before you analyze the video and award star ratings, you will want to filter the collection so that it only displays clips from, for example, the huge buffalo shot or your most recent project. Organizing files in the Organizer may be accomplished via the use of the menu bar and drop-down choices located at the top of the screen. For this reason, for example, you may use the drop-down menu to filter files by selecting "Date (Newest First)" or you can use the Find By History Imported option to see movies that were uploaded on a certain day. (You are relieved to know that you do not have to rely on your memory to recall the date. **To preview your films and provide star ratings, you should do the following activities once you have picked the right clips:**

1. Select **View Photos and Video in Full Screen** from the menu that appears after you have used the right mouse button to click on the first clip.
2. Press the **Play button.**

It is recommended that you view a video clip many times before deciding on its rating and whether or not you want to use it in any way. You should keep in mind, however, that you are not compelled to utilize the whole clip itself. It is not a good idea to throw away a clip that has some great sections since you may only need to use a little portion of it. The Auto-Analyzer feature in Premiere may be able to aid you in assessing your clips; but, for the time being, you need to be aware of what you want your film to accomplish. To provide a star rating to the video, you should view it as many times as is required.

3. Determine if the clip is appropriate by directing your mouse to the button in the Quick Edit panel that is labeled with a single star.

The rating is shown with one enormous gold star and four stars that are ghosted out respectively. It is possible to locate it in both the Organize tab of Premiere as well as the Organizer. When comparing one video clip to another, it might be difficult to do so, especially if you have not seen all of the film. Taking this into consideration, it is reasonable to reduce the bar on your first attempt. Please do not give any stars to the videos that are so terrible. Please provide videos that are suitable for one or two stars. As the number of clips decreases and the ones that have already been evaluated are reassessed, you could decide to assign a higher rating to the videos that are of greater quality.

4. Do this for each of the media clips.

The amount of video that you recorded might make it tedious to view each film more than once, depending on how much material you gathered. Always keep in mind that the time you put in the now will help you save a significant amount of time in the future. Right now, the most important thing you need to do is get rid of all of the terrible material. In the future, you will never have to see that terrible video again.

Get a Good View

When it comes to previewing video clips, both the Organizer and Premiere provide a variety of options. Depending on the type of video you are working with, you could discover that one of these tools is more efficient than the other. If you find that the Full Screen view of the Organizer **results in fuzzy clips or stuttering when playing, then you should choose one of the following options for assessing and rating clips:**

1. To begin playing the media player, right-click the clip that is located in the lightbox of the Organizer and choose the option to **Play Video or Audio.**
2. Click the **Play button** to see the preview of a video clip.
3. To close the media player, click the **X** on the top right corner of the screen.
4. Within the lightbox, provide a star rating to the video snippet. When you don't see stars beneath the thumbnails in the lightbox, you may view information by using the **Ctrl+D** key combination.
5. Choose the subsequent clip and proceed with the same process.

Preview and Rate in Premiere

It is recommended that you attempt screening and rating your video in Premiere if you are unable to utilize any of the Organizer solutions. Take the following steps:

1. To see your clips in Premiere, pick the **Organize tab**, and then click the Media button.
2. In the Media Arrangement menu, choose the tab labeled "**Newest First.**"
3. Select the **Details check box** to see the star rating for an individual clip.
4. Double-click on a clip you want to open in the Preview box.
5. If you want to make the Preview window larger, you can do so by dragging one of its corners.
6. Press the **play button** to begin watching the video in the preview.
7. To close the media player, click the X on the top-right corner of the screen.
8. Click the star rating that is located below the video to submit a rating.
9. Choose the subsequent clip and proceed with the same process.

Apply Keyword Tags to Clips

You are only able to generalize about whether a video is fairly outstanding or dreadful by using the star rating technique, which does not provide a great deal of information on the contents of the video. Both keyword tags, which are discussed in this section, and smart tags, which are discussed in the next section, provide you the opportunity to be more specific in your search results. When viewing media files in the Organizer or Premiere's Organize tab, you will only see a still frame of a clip during that viewing session. You could be inquisitive about several things, including who is in the video, where it was filmed when it was shot, and perhaps as many as a dozen other things. This allows you to filter your view in either the Organizer or the Organize tab of Premiere. Keyword tags are used for this purpose. Despite this, you need to be in the Organizer to generate tags and apply them to clips. **The way to go about it is as follows:**

1. In Premiere Elements, launch the program and choose the **Organize tab**, followed by the Organizer button. As an alternative, you have the option to choose Arrange from the splash screen of Premiere.

As soon as the Organizer application is launched, the tab labeled "Organize" is selected from the tabbed area shown on the right side of the Tasks panel. This causes your material to be displayed in the lightbox. At first, the Organizer displays all of the media files that you have. Before adding keyword tags, decrease the number of clips to a more acceptable level by using filters to minimize the number of clips.

2. If the option to **Show All** is there, you should click on it.

The Show All option is no longer available, and the Organizer now displays every item that is included inside your library. According to what you discovered in the previous section, the Show All option will only appear if the lightbox view has been filtered in the working session that is now being discussed.

3. Choose the project or album from the Albums area that includes the files that you wish to tag. Only one album or project may be chosen at a time when doing so. If you click on a name, the Organizer will only display the material that is associated with that particular project or album.

4. (This is optional) To arrange your material by the star rating, choose an option from the menu that appears after clicking a star in the upper-right-hand corner of the lightbox.

"and higher," "and lower," or "just" are the options that are available to you from the drop-down menu that appears when you click on one of the stars. For example, you may highlight the third ghosted star by clicking on it, and then make sure that the "and higher" option is selected from the menu. This will reveal all of the videos that have ratings of three stars or above.

5. Pick the videos that you wish to tag.

If you are just labeling a single clip, you may simply drag the tag to the clip without even having to make a selection first. It is possible to tag many clips at the same time using any of the typical multiple-selection techniques, including the following:

- Use the **Ctrl key** to pick many clips
- **Shift-click** to choose several related clips
- To choose a collection of clips, click and drag a selection box.

6. Choose a tag or tags to use.

There are several tag types and subclasses available in Premiere. For example, you may choose the People category, and then the video could be tagged with subcategories such as Family and Friends. If you want to apply several tags to the selected clips, you may highlight the tags by pressing the Ctrl or Shift key simultaneously.

7.   After selecting a clip, drop one of the tags onto it by dragging it.

For every one of the selected clips, the organizer assigns the relevant tags.

Create a New Keyword Tag

The Organizer is the only place where new tags can be generated. Make your selection from the Organize tab on the Task panel. Clicking the triangle symbol will allow you to open the Keyword Tags panel if it is currently closed. There are two different ways that tags may be displayed: Tag Hierarchy, which involves clicking the symbol that looks like a TV screen with a tag next to it, and Tag Cloud, which involves clicking the cloud that has a huge "T" on it. In the Tag Hierarchy, you will see tags that you may choose to only view clips that have that particular tag. You can sort the Cloud view based on a particular tag by clicking on a word in the word list. The use of Tag Hierarchy makes the process of generating a new tag easier since it allows you to examine the major categories (such as People, Places, and so on) as well as the subcategories that fall under those basic categories (for example, Family and Friends under People). During the process of generating a new tag, you may access a menu that contains the following options by clicking the big green plus sign.

New Keyword Tags: If you do this, you will be able to access the Create Keyword Tag screen and all of the options it contains. Simply clicking the Edit Icon button will allow you to choose a label, color, and icon for the new tag. This insignia is shown by Premiere on the still frame of the video, which makes it simple to view while editing the film. On the other hand, if you were to create a tag for Clementine, your basset hound, you might use a picture of her as the symbol representation. The next thing that has to be done is to indicate to Premiere where this new tag should be placed in the list of all tags. Make advantage of the Category drop-down option to include it into an existing tag as a subcategory. For example, if you want to create a tag for Clementine under the "Pets" category, you should choose the Pets category. Once you have created the tag by clicking the OK button, the name "Clementine" will display under the "Pets" heading, complete with a little picture of your hound dog already included in the tag. Additionally, you have the option of including a map and other annotations in your tag.

New Sub-Category: One of the subsets of the **New Keyword Tag option** is the New Sub-Category option, which also gives you the ability to create and insert new tags. This is a significant difference since you are unable to set a tag color or image in this context. Your newly created subcategory will take on the tag properties that were taken from the parent category. As a consequence of this, adding a subcategory to Events leads it to be shown as a red tag with a few lines of text that are completely make-believe. Considering that the New Sub-Category performs the same purpose as the one described before, you may be asking why it is even present in the list. To facilitate the creation of a tag without the need to provide a tag color or icon image, the Create Sub-Category feature is used.

New Category: At the most advanced level of keyword tags in the Elements language, a "**category**" is the designation. Individuals, locations, and events are all examples of things that may be used to represent categories. There is a subcategory that all of the following things belong to. To create a new top-level tag, choose this option, then give the category a name, and complete the process by selecting a tag color and icon.

Remove Keyword Tags

You may change your mind regarding a keyword tag as you continue to work on projects. This is not a problem; all it takes is a few clicks to do. "**Remove Clementine Keyword Tag**" is one of the options that comes in the menu that appears when you right-click on the blue keyword tag of a clip. It is important to be aware that Premiere will erase the tag as soon as you click on it; thus, you will not see a notification box to confirm your actions. When you right-click on a thumbnail, you have the option of selecting Delete Keyword Tag from the context menu. This is an alternate possibility. This method displays a submenu that contains the keyword tags in addition to the smart tags that will be detailed in the next section. Utilizing the Remove Tag option in Premiere will allow you to discover the specific tags that were applied to a clip. If you follow the instructions above, you should avoid clicking on any tags since doing so will cause them to be removed. Exiting the menu is as simple as moving your cursor to a different location on the screen and then left-clicking.

CHAPTER 15

TROUBLESHOOTING COMMON ISSUES

Troubleshoot Premiere Elements projects

Solution 1: Work on a project whose settings are appropriate for your imported files.

When trying to play a file in Adobe Premiere Elements, issues often arise when the project settings do not align with the characteristics of the imported file. Many problems might arise as a result of this discrepancy, such as distorted widescreen movies or fuzzy standard-definition files used for projects requiring other specifications. You must be familiar with the file's fundamental details to choose the optimal project parameters. A file's frame size (also termed **"Image Size"**), frame rate, and pixel aspect ratio may be quickly accessed by right-clicking on the file in the Project view and selecting **"Properties."** A popup with this information will then appear. These specifics aid users in making informed decisions on project setup. **Create a new project and adjust the settings according to these detailed instructions:**

1. Start by selecting **"New"** from the **"File"** menu, then **"Project."** Alternatively, you can access the **"New Project"** option directly from the welcome window.
2. As the **"New Project"** window appears, choose **"Change Settings."**
3. Next, a **"Setup"** box will appear; from there, you can choose the option that corresponds to your file(s)'s characteristics. Select the most similar option if none exists that precisely meets your file's requirements.
4. Click **"OK"** to confirm your selections once you've given your project a name.

To ensure that your media files playback without a hitch and maintain top quality throughout your editing projects in Adobe Premiere Elements, follow these steps to control file settings and set up project configurations.

Solution 2: Render previews of clips on the Timeline or Sceneline.

To watch imported video files more smoothly in Adobe Premiere Elements' Timeline or Sceneline, rendering previews are typically necessary. You may see the results of your previously computed clip data in the temporary files created when you render previews. Having this on hand will make playing music while you work much easier. If you want to see previews of clips in **the Work Area on the Timeline—and maybe even make things go faster—then follow these steps:**

1. **Press the Enter key**. When you press the Enter key while the Timeline or Sceneline is already open, the clips you selected will begin to render in the selected Work Area. To make viewing easier, Premiere Elements creates sample files when you do this.

2. **Working with the Timeline Menu**: You may also access the Timeline menu and choose the "**Render Work Area**" option to work with the timeline. This line of code instructs the application to show just the sample files for the Work Area that was specified on the Timeline.

Temporary files are created during teaser rendering that aid in gameplay. By adhering to these instructions, Adobe Premiere Elements may generate approximated data, which significantly enhances the playback of your edited film. You may speed up and simplify the editing process for your projects by using Adobe Premiere Elements' rendering previews to make playing video files easier as you edit.

Solution 3: Adjust the scaling, frame rate, pixel aspect ratio, or field settings.

If you're still experiencing issues after attempting Solutions 1 and 2, the following additional actions may be of assistance:

1. **Adjusting Video Size**: Selecting the Clip on the Timeline or Scenery will allow you to change the video's size if it doesn't fit the screen or is excessively enlarged. After that, find the "**Clip**" menu, then choose "**Video Options**," and lastly, "**Scale to Frame Size**." This will guarantee that the video clip is appropriately adjusted to suit the frame without compromising quality.

2. **Changing the Pixel Aspect Ratio**: If the loaded video seems compressed or distorted, Adobe Premiere Elements may be misunderstanding the pixel aspect ratio of the file. To resolve this issue, use the "Interpret Footage" function. The accurate rendering and display of the video depends on the pixel aspect ratio, which may be adjusted using this command.

3. **Changing the Playback Speed and Frame Rate**: If the imported video still plays at an incorrect frame rate or stutters after creating samples, it's likely because Adobe Premiere Elements is misinterpreting the frame rate. As a solution, you might use the "**Interpret Footage**" tool. Find the file in the Project view, right-click on it, and then choose "**Interpret Footage.**" Here you can adjust the playback speed and set the proper frame rate.

Note: There will be continuous stuttering if the frame rate is fifteen frames per second or below.

4. **Correcting Interlaced Video Playback:** When playing back imported interlaced video files, Adobe Premiere Elements may be erroneously reading the field order, resulting in jagged edges, and thin horizontal lines (referred to as "combing") on moving objects or flickering. If you use the "**Interpret Footage**" tool to appropriately change the field order, you can remedy this. Additional options for fine-tuning and resolving field-order issues may be found in the Field Options panel.

While editing video in Adobe Premiere Elements, you may repair a broad variety of playback difficulties using these all-around strategies and the Interpret Footage command. This will ensure that your video material is displayed more precisely and smoothly.

Troubleshoot file formats and codecs

Adobe Premiere Elements and other video recording and editing applications employ common file formats such as AVI, MOV, and WMV to convert video files. Make sure you know whether these file formats are compatible with Adobe Premiere Elements for a pleasant editing experience. Finding all the file formats compatible with your Adobe Premiere Elements version is as easy as browsing the Adobe Knowledgebase for "**Supported file formats in Adobe Premiere Elements <your version>.**" Formats like AVI and MOV are containers for video files, so keep that in mind. Package contents are encoded using certain codecs. Aptly named **"coder-decoder,"** codecs are the tools used to reduce the file sizes of media files. The file size and quality may be altered by using various codecs, which compress data in different ways. An AVI file, for instance, might use a variety of codecs, including the DV codec (often used by miniDV camcorders), the Motion JPEG codec, or even a commercial codec like DivX. Some still-image cameras can capture video using the Motion JPEG format as well. Video files compressed using poorly designed or incompatible codecs may not play properly in Adobe Premiere Elements. Because of this restriction, the program may have trouble properly understanding and editing the video material, which might lead to interface issues. Make sure the codecs used to compress video files are generally recognized and compatible with Adobe Premiere Elements to prevent any issues with decoding. Typically, resolving these compatibility issues may be as simple as downloading the necessary codecs or converting the files to a format that Adobe Premiere Elements is compatible with. To use the correct techniques, you must be familiar with the video files' format and, if applicable, codec. **To get this crucial data, you may want to consider the following options:**

1. **Using Apple QuickTime Player**: To see the video, use Apple QuickTime Player, provided you have access to the file. After that, open the video's properties (file type, codec, size, frame rate, etc.) by selecting "**Show Movie Inspector**" from the "**Window**" menu.

2. **Referring to Device Documentation**: When looking for video files that originated from camcorders, cameras, or any other recording equipment, it's a good idea to consult the manual that came with the specific model. You can usually learn a lot about the recording's file format and codec from these papers. The manufacturer's website is another good place to see the device's specifications; there, you'll likely discover details on the file formats and codecs that the device is compatible with.

3. **Utilizing Third-Party Programs**: Using Third-Party Software: Make use of third-party software specifically designed to analyze media files, such as **MediaInfo or GSpot 2.70.** Use these tools to open the video file and learn more about its codec, features, bitrates,

format, and audio/video components. You may learn everything about the file's encoding details using these applications.

By following these steps, you will be well-versed in identifying video files by type and codec. This data is vital for resolving issues and selecting appropriate solutions when dealing with media in Adobe Premiere Elements.

Solution 4: Install a required codec.

Common video codecs used for compression include DivX, Xvid, 3ivx, and others; however, they may not be installed on standard Windows or Apple QuickTime installations. This means that your computer may not be able to open certain file formats until you obtain and install additional codecs. To play AVI files encoded with the DivX format in media players like Windows Media Player, for instance, you need to install the DivX codec. Media player software can often play files created with a certain codec after loading the appropriate codec. It could also be useful for fixing issues with certain file formats in Adobe Premiere Elements. However, remember that installing a codec isn't a guarantee that Adobe Premiere Elements will work flawlessly every time you import or play a file. More sophisticated hardware is required for the application to edit video files rather than just play them. This means that, as mentioned in Solution 6, challenging files will need to be transcoded (converted) if issues persist. The websites of software companies often include download links for codecs. It is crucial to use caution while obtaining codecs, however. Only download codecs from reputable software developers to guarantee stability and security. Do not install software packages labeled "codec pack" since doing so can lead to unanticipated issues. Remember that certain media files may become inaccessible after installing a new codec. This is why it's crucial to back up your data before installing any codecs.

Solution 5: Remove one or more installed codecs.

Installing a poorly made codec might be the cause of your problems while trying to save or play files of the same type from various sources. This problem might also arise if there are conflicting codecs loaded for the same video file. The removal or blocking of third-party codecs is one solution to these codec problems. To uninstall certain codecs, particularly those that were part of a "codec pack" download, utilize Windows XP's "Add or Remove Programs" or Vista's "Programs and Features" menu items. However, you can't just delete codecs from the Control Panel. Additional measures may be required in this instance. **For further instructions on how to disable or remove additional installed codecs, you may refer to the following TechNotes for certain Windows versions:**
- **For Windows XP:**
  - Temporarily disable a codec (kb404870)
  - Remove a codec (kb404869)
- **For Windows Vista:**

- Temporarily disable a codec (kb404892)

By adhering to these guidelines, you should be able to steer clear of issues caused by incompatible or inappropriate codecs. Playing and working with files from many sources that share comparable formats should be made simpler by this.

Solution 6: Transcode problematic video files.

If you are unable to save or view a video file in Adobe Premiere Elements, you may be able to fix this by using a different program to convert or alter the file. You may import the transcoded files into Premiere Elements for easier editing and playback thereafter. Transcoding is the process of converting a file format to another. It is possible to transcode files that use the same format, such as converting 3ivx-encoded AVI files to DV-encoded AVI files. Altering the format is another option; for example, you can convert a VOB file to an AVI file. To maintain the highest possible picture quality when converting, it is recommended to choose a raw or low-compression output option in your program. There are a plethora of Windows conversion applications. **The following is an incomplete list of possibilities; still, you may find that other applications are more suited to your needs:**
- HandBrake.
- VLC Media Player.
- FFmpeg.
- Any Video Converter.
- Format Factory.

In case you didn't know, Adobe doesn't endorse or support third-party applications. We only provide the program list as a service. It is recommended that you contact the software's developer or review their instructions if you need assistance with any of these third-party translation tools. To address interface issues and make your video files more usable in Adobe Premiere Elements, choosing the correct encoding software is crucial.
- **AVI files:** VirtualDub; Microsoft Windows Movie Maker.
- **QuickTime (MOV) and MPEG-4 files:** Apple QuickTime Player for Windows with QuickTime Pro.
- **MPEG-2 and VOB files:** MPEG Streamclip; Apple QuickTime Player for Windows with QuickTime Pro and MPEG-2 Playback Component.

Troubleshoot video playback issues

Viewing and speed issues are possible with Premiere Elements. Issues that often arise include:
- Drop-in frames (choppy or jerky playback)
- Audio drop out
- No Video during playback
- Playback gets stuck when you hit the play button or spacebar

To resolve the most frequent starting problems, follow these instructions. Keep reading if the problem persists after you've tried these solutions.

Check if your system meets the minimum system requirements.

Note: To examine fundamental system specs like the installed RAM and CPU speed.
- On Windows, go to **Start**, then **Control Panel**, and finally **System**.
- Locate the Apple logo in macOS and click on it in the upper left corner. Select **About This Mac** from the menu.

Try these solutions first

- Verify that the program you're using can open the file, not only Adobe. You can see whether it works by opening the file in a different media player on your PC.
- Make sure the video card driver is up-to-date. Motion video and graphics may not display correctly if the video card drivers are outdated or damaged. Another possibility is that they may incorrectly instruct Adobe Premiere Elements to display motion video or effects. Simply contact the manufacturer of your video card or visit their website to get the latest driver version. By examining the characteristics of a video card in Device Manager, you may determine its manufacturer.
- Use only one screen for a little while. Put another way, consolidate your computing needs into one.
- A third-party adaptor may modify the file type so that your computer's operating system can read it.

Render all effects, transitions, and titles in the Timeline.

To guarantee flawless playback, it is sometimes necessary to render media files. Adobe Premiere components make an effort to play undrawn components in real-time without rendering them beforehand. This includes effects, transitions, titles, and more. Your computer's real-time music-playing capabilities are CPU and resource-dependent. By displaying the Timeline's unrendered media items, you may reduce the system's reliance on its resources. As you work, you can see how well the playback is doing for only the section of the timeline that you're now focusing on. Changing this is as simple as dragging the timeline's work area bar.

Troubleshooting playback issues related to audio hardware

1. Go to **Edit > Preferences > Audio Hardware** to see the audio hardware and settings that Premiere Elements is using for playing and recording. Here you may see the CoreAudio settings on macOS, and the ASIO and MME settings on Windows.

2. Try to identify and disable any external microphones or sound sources. For example, you have the option to disable the camera, USB microphones, and any third-party audio-playing devices such as AJA or BlackMagic.
3. Try utilizing one of the in-built input/output devices to create an aggregate device on macOS.

To see if it helps, in Windows go to the Sounds menu and disable all the devices except Realtek.

Disconnect all peripheral devices except the digital video device

Connecting a device to a computer via a USB, serial, SCSI, parallel, or FireWire connection could halt video playback if the driver requests system resources. Peripheral devices include things like printers, scanners, modems, and network connections. To reduce the demands placed on the system by the media player, disable or unplug any auxiliary devices. Additionally, you may only use one device at a time on a FireWire card or chain with Adobe Premiere Elements. **Note**: Even after you remove the cables, the network standards will remain in effect until you power cycle the machine.

Optimize the project settings

Check if the clip's characteristics, such as frame rate, data rate, and compression, are compatible with the project parameters. If your project contains many pieces of media, be sure to choose the project parameters that are compatible with each clip. The project file should be located on the quickest hard drive, and all of the samples and clips should be on the same disk as well. **Edit > Preferences > Scratch Disks** is where you can find the option to adjust the scratch drive configuration in Adobe Premiere Elements.

Turn on/off Intel Hardware Acceleration

Occasionally, adjusting the Intel Hardware options will resolve issues with Premiere Elements' playback. **To modify Intel Hardware Acceleration settings, follow these steps:**
On the Windows platform:
1. Select **Edit**, followed by **Preferences**, and lastly **General**.
2. For Intel HD Graphics 2000 and later, disable the Use Hardware Acceleration option.
3. Launch the application once again.

For macOS:
1. Go to "**Preferences**" and choose "**General**."
2. For Intel HD Graphics 2000 and later, disable the Use Hardware Acceleration option.
3. Launch the application once again.

You should also update your display drivers if modifying the Intel Hardware Settings resolves the issue.

Change playback quality for better quality/performance

Select "playing quality" from the context menu to adjust the audio volume. **To enhance the playback quality, choose one of these options:**

1. Automatic
2. Highest
3. Medium
4. Lowest

Check for device driver problems

Video display adapters, SCSI and IDE controller cards, motherboard BIOS and chipsets, and other hardware components may communicate with Windows using device drivers. Receive in touch with the computer or device manufacturer to receive the most recent driver software.

Disable non-essential startup items and services

Adobe Premiere Elements may encounter conflicts or resource conflicts with other Windows-bundled applications and services, such as antivirus, firewall, and anti-crash programs. To temporarily disable the operation of unused startup items and services, you may use the Windows System Configuration Utility.

Follow these steps to launch Windows in a streamlined mode:

1. **Close All Apps**: Close or stop all open programs to make the transition to basic mode easier.
2. **Access System Configuration Utility (msconfig):** To open Windows System Configuration Utility, just type "msconfig" into the Windows context menu:

Press the "**Start**" button. Choose "**Run**" from the list. On the other hand, you can just put it into the search bar in newer versions of Windows.

Press OK or Enter after typing "msconfig" into the box.

3. **Note down the Deselected Items**: In the System Configuration Utility, go to the "**Startup**" and "**Services**" tabs to make a note of the items that have been chosen. Currently, under these headings, make a note of anything that is not selected or ticked. When you boot into basic mode, these items reveal which programs and services are unable to launch.
4. **Choose Selective Startup:** Launch the System Configuration Utility, and then go to the "**General**" page to choose Selective Startup. The "**Selective Startup**" option should be chosen. You may choose the various system beginning components here.
5. **Disable All Startup Items:** Stop Most programs from Starting up with Computer Startup: To stop all startup items from running automatically, go to the "**Startup**" menu and choose "**Disable All**." This should do the trick for most programs.

6. **Hide All Microsoft Services**: To hide all Microsoft services and display just third-party ones, go to the "**Services**" tab and tick the box that reads "**Hide All Microsoft Services**." This will conceal all of Microsoft's relevant services.

7. **Turn off non-Microsoft services**: To prevent non-Microsoft services from launching during system startup, click "Disable All" on the "Services" menu. Remember to re-enable or re-select the "FLEXnet Licensing Service." It's recommended to keep a service turned off if you're unsure of its need.

8. **Restart and Apply Changes**: After you've finished editing the system configuration, click "Apply" in the box that appears. Then, restart your computer. The next step is to restart your computer to apply the modifications. Windows will launch in a stripped-down mode with only the most essential Microsoft services and a handful of startup programs when you power up your machine again.

You can address issues caused by third-party applications or services by starting Windows in this simplified mode, which improves the beginning environment. It should be noted that the System Configuration tool has altered Windows' startup behavior, and you will be notified of this upon restart. As soon as the System Configuration tool appears, click Cancel, and then click OK again.

- To stop or disable any currently running beginning processes, just right-click on an icon in the Notification Area.
- You have transferred the Adobe Premiere Elements folder to your computer's desktop. Locate the setup.exe file in that folder and double-click on it.

The next step is to replicate the issue:

- One of the startup processes is incompatible with Adobe Premiere Elements, even if the issue disappears. Find the one that doesn't function with Adobe Premiere Elements by re-enabling beginning things one by one and testing each one. To find out whether there is any new information; contact the creator of that item.
- You may turn the initial items back on if the issue returns; they are not to fault.

Follow these procedures to enable setting things up again:

1. Choose "**Start**" and then "**Run**." In the "Open" box, enter "**msconfig**." Finally, hit **OK**.
2. On the **General** tab, choose **Normal Startup**.
3. You can go back to Step 3 of the previous section and cross out whatever you marked.
4. After clicking "**Apply**" and restarting Windows, the modifications will be visible.

Test playback on an external device

Find out how well the hard drive functions by using a third-party program, such as Canopus EZDVtest or TCD Labs HDTach. Adobe recommends that hard disks fulfill these specifications.

To play back HDV media:

- It is recommended to have at least two 80 GB SATA drives with a 7200 RPM UDMA 133 interface set up in Zero Raid mode, or

- A large 7200 RPM UDMA 133 IDE, SATA, or SCSI hard drive capable of maintaining rates of 20 MB/s or more

To play 4K or Full HD media:

- A dedicated 7200 RPM SATA hard drive with plenty of storage capacity and the ability to maintain rates of 150 MB/second or higher
- Use Solid State Drives (SSDs) if you're editing in 4K or Full HD. The usage of an SDD allows for the rapid handling, opening, and display of files. Data transmission rates range from 300 MB/s to 40 GB/s.

Optimize hard disks

Clean hard drives, current drivers, and proper disk drive setup will improve Adobe Premiere Elements' performance and playback speed. Get in touch with the gear manufacturer or a certified repair shop if you want any more assistance with these tasks.

- To defragment your hard drives, you may use Windows' built-in Disk Defragmenter or an external program like Symantec Norton Utilities. You have the option to utilize external drives for video, even if they aren't part of your system. A disk's data is permanently deleted during the conversion process. If you are unsure about how to perform anything, see the utility's manual or Windows Help.
- Keeping the disk drivers up-to-date will prevent them from being corrupted or incompatible with your computer. You should use the program that was used to prepare the disk if it was prepared using another disk tool. To find out how to use the tool, read the instructions that came with it.
- **Get the hard drive's write cache up and running:**
  - Make a search for Device Manager in the search bar.
  - To add a disk drive, click the plus sign (+).
  - Click the hard drive twice.
  - Click the Policies tab in the Disk Device Properties box.
  - Choose to allow disk write caching.
- Please ensure that any additional IDE (or EIDE) disks that you want to utilize for video editing are connected to the second driver. The primary controller should only receive IDE disks. Connecting all other devices to the main controller is also necessary. The backup processor can transfer data at maximum speed when only IDE drives are connected to it. Data rates are limited by the maximum speeds that slower devices can manage while connected to the same network. When compared to hard disks used for video editing, their data transfer speeds are often lower. You can find instructions on how to link disks to a driver in the computer's documentation.

Conclusion

If you want to be an expert with this video editing program, you need to know how to utilize all of its functions, from the most basic to the most complex, and how to put together polished projects quickly and easily. Video editing may be intimidating for newcomers, but Premiere Elements makes it easy for even the most inexperienced users to create professional-quality films with ease. Mastering the project panel, animating with keyframes, applying slow-motion and time-lapse effects, and deciphering file formats and codecs are all features and tools that will help you create exceptional material. You can create consistently high-quality films with engaging stories by using the information and methods provided in this tutorial. Keep trying new things and don't be afraid to experiment with different effects as you learn to edit more quickly. Because of its intuitive design, Premiere Elements streamlines the editing process so that you can give more attention to realizing your ideas and less to the technical details. If you want to see your editing confidence and creativity soar, all you have to do is keep challenging yourself to improve.

INDEX

T

Made in the USA
Las Vegas, NV
06 January 2025

15930616R00122